Window Treatments & Slipcovers

FOR DUMMIES®

by Mark Montano and Carly Sommerstein

WILEY

Wiley Publishing, Inc.

Window Treatments & Slipcovers For Dummies®

Published by
Wiley Publishing, Inc.
111 River St.
Hoboken, NJ 07030-5774
www.wiley.com

Copyright © 2006 by Wiley Publishing, Inc., Indianapolis, Indiana

Published simultaneously in Canada

For general information on our other products and services, please contact our Customer Care Department within the U.S. at 800-762-2974, outside the U.S. at 317-572-3993, or fax 317-572-4002.

For technical support, please visit www.wiley.com/techsupport.

Wiley also publishes its books in a variety of electronic formats. Some content that appears in print may not be available in electronic books.

Library of Congress Control Number: 2005924594

ISBN-13: 978-0-7645-8448-0

ISBN-10: 0-7645-8448-0

Manufactured in the United States of America

10 9 8 7 6 5 4 3 2 1

1O/RZ/RQ/QV/IN

WILEY

About the Authors

Mark Montano is best known as the lead designer on *While You Were Out*, the hit designing show on TLC, which he joined in 2003. It's one of the most-recognized and best-loved home redesign shows on television.

Well before *While You Were Out*, Mark began designing clothing for his mother at the age of 14. After graduating from Colorado State University (where he earned a bachelor's degree in business), Mark moved to New York City, where he continued his education at the Fashion Institute of Technology, earning a master's degree in costume history. An internship at Oscar de la Renta gave him an appreciation for exquisite fabrics and the inspiration to begin his own clothing line.

He opened his flagship boutique in New York's East Village and established himself in the world of haute couture. As the youngest member ever to be inducted into the Council of Fashion Designers of America, Mark designed a signature collection of ready-to-wear and custom couture for more than ten years, which was shown to great acclaim on the runways of New York's Fashion Week.

Mark joined the staff of *Cosmo Girl!* magazine as a contributing editor in 1999, where he began a monthly room makeover column called "Cool Room." In early 2002, Mark continued inspiring teens with the publication of his first book, *Super Suite,* a collection of room makeovers for 15 teenage girls, which was selected for inclusion in the "Books for the Teen Age 2003 List," published by the New York Public Library.

He also writes a weekly column entitled "Make Your Mark," syndicated in more than 70 newspapers by Knight Ridder, in which he answers a wide range of readers' decorating questions. In August 2004, Mark began work as a feature columnist in the New York Post's home section, where his column "Mark Your Territory" tackles city-living design problems.

Mark's book, *Dollar Store Décor,* was published to great acclaim in 2005, and he's currently hard at work on a new TV show, TLC's *10 Years Younger.* He lives in New York City and Los Angeles.

Carly Sommerstein attended New York University, where she studied English and American literature. She has worked as a freelance book editor for more than 13 years. Her writing has appeared in the *NY Press,* the *Utne Reader,* *Jane,* www.playboy.com, and elsewhere. She also collaborated with Mark Montano on *Super Suite.* Carly lives in the New York City area with her husband and two-year-old son.

Dedication

This book is dedicated to our loved ones, and to everyone who has the desire to make things more beautiful.

Authors' Acknowledgments

So many people had a hand in creating this book, and we want to extend our deepest thanks and lasting gratitude to every one of them. Thank you, Diane Graves Steele, vice president and publisher, and Mikal Belicove, acquisitions editor, for coming up with the concept for the book and for giving us the chance to execute it. Thanks to Janet Rosen, our adorable and energetic agent, and Sheree Bykofsky of Sheree Bykofsky Associates, for their faith and on-going moral support. The great Jeremy Nelson did the interior photography, and the fine folks at Kreber in Columbus, Ohio, provided the color-insert photos; thanks and kudos to you both. Many thanks to the graphics department at Wiley, who created this book's line drawings.

The project editors and copyeditors of the publishing world are rarely given their fair due. These diligent, highly organized, and creative multitaskers contribute hugely to the final product. Thank you, Chrissy Guthrie and Sherri Pfouts, for your amazing brains and for your dedication and encouragement during the shaping of this book from start to finish. Copyeditors Chad Sievers and Neil Johnson corrected our spelling and syntax and made many smart comments and suggestions that helped a great deal. We also want to acknowledge the helpful contribution of our technical editors, Carol Spier and Sandra Rea, for going behind our work and pointing us in the right direction.

Mark thanks his parents for helping him to think out of the box, Jorge Montano for his organizational skills and good cheer, and his cowriter Carly Sommerstein.

Carly thanks her late grandmother Betty Liner, a talented seamstress and fabric lover who first exposed her to creativity with cloth. Thanks to her husband, J.R. Taylor, for his unconditional love and support. She also thanks her mother-in-law, baby genius Barbara Taylor, and Sherylann Matthias, her amazing nanny, who both helped to care for her son, Judah Ray Taylor, during the writing of this book; it truly does take a village. And thank you, Mark Montano, for your sense of humor and giant talent. It's a pleasure to work with you and an honor to be your friend.

Publisher's Acknowledgments

We're proud of this book; please send us your comments through our Dummies online registration form located at www.dummies.com/register/.

Some of the people who helped bring this book to market include the following:

Acquisitions, Editorial, and Media Development

Project Editors: Sherri Pfouts, Christina Guthrie

Acquisitions Editor: Mikal Belicove

Copy Editors: Chad Sievers, Neil Johnson

Editorial Program Assistant: Courtney Allen

Technical Editors: Carol Spier, Sandra Rea

Editorial Manager: Christine Meloy Beck

Editorial Assistants: Hanna Scott, Nadine Bell

Cover Photos: © Ira Montgomery/ Getty Images/The Image Bank

Cartoons: Rich Tennant (www.the5thwave.com)

Composition Services

Project Coordinator: Adrienne Martinez

Layout and Graphics: Jonelle Burns, Brian Drumm, Kelly Emkow, Joyce Haughey, Stephanie D. Jumper, Barbara Moore, Barry Offringa, Brent Savage, Amanda Spagnuolo, Julie Trippetti

Special Art: Color section photos by Mark Madden, Kreber; in-text photos by Jeremy Nelson

Proofreaders: Leeann Harney, Jessica Kramer, TECHBOOKS Production Services

Indexer: TECHBOOKS Production Services

Publishing and Editorial for Consumer Dummies

    Diane Graves Steele, Vice President and Publisher, Consumer Dummies

    Joyce Pepple, Acquisitions Director, Consumer Dummies

    Kristin A. Cocks, Product Development Director, Consumer Dummies

    Michael Spring, Vice President and Publisher, Travel

    Kelly Regan, Editorial Director, Travel

Publishing for Technology Dummies

    Andy Cummings, Vice President and Publisher, Dummies Technology/General User

Composition Services

    Gerry Fahey, Vice President of Production Services

    Debbie Stailey, Director of Composition Services

Contents at a Glance

Table of Contents

Introduction

We're delighted to welcome you to our take on window treatment and slipcover design. If you're bored with what's being offered to you in the stores and want to take a crack at doing it yourself, you came to the right place. We think making your own window treatments and slipcovers is the perfect way to express your individual style, to make a room truly special and entirely your own. This book provides you with our formula for a little style magic: We provide several fun ideas to jazz up your windows and furniture and explain step by step how to make them come to life. All you need is some money, time, and effort, and before you know it, you'll be creating beautiful window treatments and slipcovers for which you'd pay an interior decorator a king's ransom (not to mention bragging rights!).

As soon as you get the do-it-yourself bug, don't be surprised if you scoff out loud at all the store-bought home decorating products, their inflated prices, and their listless design quality.

About This Book

Window Treatments & Slipcovers For Dummies is a book for everyone — from those of you who don't own a sewing machine, and don't want to, to those who are learning the ins and outs of sewing, to those of you who have some good basic sewing knowledge that you want to flex a bit, to those of you who have been sewing for years and want to pick up a few new design ideas. We include useful background knowledge and practical information on choosing materials (such as fabrics, trims, and hardware), tips on planning your construction, as well dozens of step-by-step projects that you can create as is, or adapt to your design needs.

We wrote this book so you can make window treatments and slipcovers easily at home and in the style you love. We conceived and translated into writing many projects that don't require any sewing knowledge, for those who want to create without sewing, and many projects that only require rudimentary sewing knowledge. We wish we had the time and space to give you a sewing tutorial for each project, but that just wasn't possible. If you want to attempt an "advanced" sewing project that we offer, but feel that your sewing skills aren't quite up to snuff, we encourage you to pick up Jan Saunders Maresh's *Sewing For Dummies,* 2nd Edition, (Wiley) which shows you all the basic step-by-step sewing concepts and techniques, and some fun projects, as well.

Conventions Used in This Book

We want to take a minute to point out some conventions we used when writing this book:

- ✔ To get you started on the right foot, each project begins with a formula for figuring out how much fabric you need to cover your particular window or piece of furniture. We also always provide an example, so that you can see the math in action.

- ✔ In addition to addressing fabric needs upfront, we also provide a list of needed tools and materials before each project. We arrange these lists of supplies alphabetically, not in their order of importance. Making sure you have all your tools and supplies handy before you begin a project is essential.

- ✔ We simplify many standard sewing practices to make this book as accessible and easy as we possibly can. If you've been taught to sew in a way that contradicts our advice, certainly do what makes you the most comfortable. But consider trying it our way. We've thought it all through, and we believe our suggestions will work out great for you and your room. Mark has been sewing for decades and really knows his stuff!

- ✔ Anytime we introduce a new sewing, fabric, or decor term, we *italicize* it.

- ✔ We **bold** all keywords as well as the steps in a numbered list.

- ✔ Web sites and e-mail addresses appear in `monofont` to help them stand out.

What You're Not to Read

Of course, we'd love for you to read each and every word of this wonderful book — after all, we wrote it! However, if you're not interested in all the details and just want to get to the heart of each project, you can skip the sidebars, which are shaded gray. Sidebars contain good-to-know but nonessential info, so they're totally skippable if you want to do so.

Also, any paragraphs marked with the Nice to Have icon are skippable as well. These paragraphs point out tools and gear that are (you guessed it) nice to have but not necessary to complete the project successfully.

Foolish Assumptions

As we wrote this book, we made some assumptions about you and your needs:

- ✔ You want to be able to create great-looking rooms without having to first achieve seamstress status. (Although for some projects in this book, we do assume that you at least know your way around a sewing machine.)

- ✔ You want a wide range of style choices to fit many different rooms.

- ✔ You're looking for tips, shortcuts, tricks, and smart advice — from soup to nuts — to lower your frustration level down to zero (or at least pretty close to zero).

- ✔ You want to start making window treatment and/or slipcover projects to spiff up your rooms right away.

If any of these assumptions fit the bill for you, welcome to our world and to this book!

How This Book Is Organized

We organized this book into five parts so that you can quickly and easily find what you want.

Part I: Window Treatments & Slipcovers 101

In this part, we talk about planning your window and slipcover projects including how to determine your style, your color likes and dislikes, your fabric choices and where to shop for them, and information on hardware and "softwear" for your windows and furniture. We also give advice on what tools you need and how to create a useful workspace.

Part II: Window Treatments in a Snap

The chapters in this part deal exclusively with the easiest no-sew and low-sew window treatments — everything you need to know about measuring, cutting, and creating simple curtains, draperies, and shades. We cover the wonderful world of window treatment accessorizing, so you can personalize your creations. We also offer some helpful timesaving shortcuts and quick fixes in case you find yourself in a jam.

Part III: Slipcovers Made Easy

This part shows you all about simple no-sew or low-sew slipcovers and how to calculate your fabric needs and measure properly so you can cover nearly any piece of furniture in your home. We offer some advice on adding accessories, such as trims and other add-ons, to your slipcovers and, as in Part II, a few shortcuts and plenty of advice on how to melt away mistakes.

Part IV: Challenging Projects to Try

Here we offer you four more chapters of window treatment and slipcover projects. Two are "intermediate" in nature; we assume you have some sewing skills that you'll use to make treatments and slipcovers that are a step up from the really easy ones in Parts II and III. We also include two more-challenging chapters for "advanced" window treatments and slipcovers.

Part V: The Part of Tens

In this part, we give you some practical style advice including our humble opinions on design tips to help you create a truly special room, as well as interior design rules that should be broken (we ardently believe that thinking outside of the box is the first step toward discovering your creativity). We also offer you a few Web resources so you can find the materials you need at a great price.

Icons Used in This Book

Throughout this book, we use icons in the margin to guide you toward important points and concepts. Here's how they break down:

Some tools are essential in creating the projects in this book, and others while not totally necessary are still nice to have. Check out the information that appears near this icon; you may find some great timesavers and frustration-savers.

This icon alerts you to useful information. This information can help guide you along the creative process as well.

The information next to this icon tells you how to do something in the quickest and best possible way.

Make sure you read the text next to this icon. We point it out to help you avoid various pitfalls and keep your sanity while you're making a project.

Where to Go from Here

Because each chapter in this book can stand on its own, you can really start anywhere you prefer. If you want to start with a window treatment, go to Part II or Part IV. If you'd rather tackle a slipcover, head to Part III or IV. And if you're the type of person who really likes to have his or her ducks in a row before beginning a project, peruse Part I to make sure you know about buying and using the right fabrics and hardware, assembling a sewing kit, and creating a functional workspace.

We do suggest that you read Chapters 2, 4, and 6 before you decide on a window treatment and Chapters 2 and 10 before you decide on a slipcover. Thinking about what kind of fabric you need and understanding some of the measuring challenges (and for window treatments, what kind of hardware to buy) go a long way toward helping you plan your project. After that, you can jump around from chapter to chapter to see which projects match your skill level as well as projects that meet your particular design needs.

Part I
Window Treatments & Slipcovers 101

The 5th Wave   By Rich Tennant

"I was thinking of making a pretty floral slipcover with ruffles for this, but I didn't want to send mixed signals."

In this part . . .

Planning your new window treatment or slipcover — or both — and getting all the materials and your workspace together may seem demanding, but we're going to make sure it's also fun. Furthermore, we promise that if you take everything one step at a time, you'll discover your hidden designer *and* see your project through from beginning to end.

In this part, we start off with some style and design choices to mull over, recommend where to go for inspiration so you can start fleshing out your projects, and provide a quick overview of construction techniques and advice on organizing a simple workspace. We tell you all you need to know about choosing, shopping for, and pretreating fabric; deciding on accessories and trims; and picking (and even making) complementary hardware and mounting it correctly. We also recommend some helpful tools that you want to keep around to make your sewing life a lot easier — and fun.

Chapter 1

Covering the Basics Before You Start

In This Chapter

▶ Thinking about color, print, scale, and texture

▶ Searching for inspiration everywhere

▶ Choosing your construction

▶ Creating a workspace and gathering your supplies

"**B**ut where do I start?" Many people, even design professionals, have uttered this phrase when faced with starting a designing endeavor. Creating something seemingly out of thin air can seem daunting, and you may even put off starting your project because you feel overwhelmed by everything. Don't worry, we're here to help.

This chapter offers some basic information and helpful tips to keep in mind when you're beginning to think about slipcover and window treatment projects you want to make. From choosing fabric to seeking out style ideas, to thinking about trims and considering whether to sew or not to sew, to organizing your workspace and getting your sewing kit together, this chapter is a great place to start — from the beginning!

Thinking about Color

Do you like light-colored, sheer fabrics for an open breezy feel? Do you like bursts of saturated color? Are you attracted to the richness of velvet? Fabrics have unique qualities that can help you express your true style (see Chapter 2 for more).

One of the first things you think about when starting a new design project is your color choice. Whether you like or dislike colors and combinations of colors is subjective, but you can rely on a few principles to help you decide what color/colors work best for your project.

Using the color spectrum

The *color spectrum* comprises the colors of a rainbow. If you remember your high school science or art classes, you may recall old Roy G. Biv, which stands for red, orange, yellow, green, blue, indigo, and violet. The warm colors — red, orange, and yellow — register in many people's eyes as advancing. They make an area look larger, tend to impart energy and vigor, and are at the left side of the color spectrum. The cool ones — green, blue, indigo, and violet — register in many people's eyes as receding. They make an area look smaller, tend to impart calm and relaxation, and are on the right side of the spectrum.

Black and white are "color-free" colors that go well with warm or cool hues. Neutrals like beige, tan, cream, and wheat can also be combined beautifully with either warm or cool hues.

Deciding whether to go cool or warm

Most people choose either warm or cool tones, and stay within the one family of colors — for example, robin's egg blue matched with indigo — which decorators call a *monochromatic* color scheme, depending on what kind of feeling they want to impart in the room. Warm tones impart a bright, happy, stimulating feeling, while cool tones give a calming, relaxing tone. Bedrooms are rooms where you relax and sleep, so many people favor cool colors, like blue, while a den and kitchen are livelier spaces that oftentimes benefit from a warmer palette. Dining rooms are often red, which is considered an appetite stimulant.

Mixing it up by choosing both

No rule says that you have to stay exclusively within the cool tones or the warm tones. In fact, we wholeheartedly advocate using both sides of the color spectrum — what we call the *cool/warm paradigm*. For example, a warm orange and a cool/neutral tan always look great together, as do a sunny yellow and a cool blue. Another winning combination is red (or pink) and gray, or blue and orange.

We encourage you to add color to your life in ways that please you. But moving all over the color spectrum with four or five colors that don't relate to one another may make the room a bit too busy, creating a space where working or relaxing is difficult. Stick to two or three compatible colors and you'll never go wrong.

Say your existing decor features a brick-red sofa, a white armchair, a light green rug, and off-white walls. You have one warm element (red), two neutral elements (white and off-white), and one cool element (green) in your room. You may decide that you want to move toward the cool family, playing up the carpet's color by incorporating another cool tone in your window treatment, say, a window treatment in a similar green, or a blue with green tones. Or you may want to move your decor toward a warmer palette by choosing a cinnamon brown slipcover fabric to cover the armchair. Saffron is another color that looks gorgeous added to warm tones.

 Paint samples, the kind on paper that you get at the hardware or paint store, are very useful to keep specific colors, or families of colors, handy when you fabric shop. Take a few home and match them to the elements of your decor you want to keep in mind when you shop. Staple 'em right into a notebook where you can easily locate them. (Check out "Nearer to thee (your references, that is)" later in this chapter and Chapter 2 for more on creating a notebook.)

Are you feeling it?

When selecting a fabric for your project , you want to consider how the fabric feels. Some fabric has a shiny finish, some is silky, some is rough, and some is a bit scratchy (see Chapter 2 for more on choosing fabric). How does the fabric feel when you sit on it, lounge on it, and touch it with your bare feet? Do your family members, especially children, who tend to have more sensitive skin, like it? At the same time that you're evaluating the feel of the fabric, consider its "hand"; how does the fabric handle, drape, or crease? Is it stiff or flimsy?

Although the fabric's feel applies more to slipcovers than to window treatments, it's still important for both types of projects that you enjoy handling the fabric while you're making your project, because that's half the fun.

Picking prints

Prints, including stripes, polka dots, florals, geometric shapes, plaids, paisleys, sunbursts, and so on, are a terrific way to add pizzazz to a room. Choose a print whose background color echoes another color in your decor to give your project and room an extra punch.

When selecting a pattern, consider contrasting its scale with other patterns in the room. *Scale* refers to the size of the patterns and how they relate to other patterns in the room. Add a small check to a large floral print for a traditional look. Mix a medium stripe with a small geometric print for a great-looking modern design scheme.

We especially love bold prints with large motifs and recommend them if they fit your decor. Large prints can provide a nice focal point to your room, like a design exclamation point. However, they can be a challenge to sew because you have to match the repeated motif across fabric panels (see Chapter 6 for more on repeats).

What's that smell?

Most people don't think about the scent of fabrics, but if you're using a certain fabric to make a slipcover you'll be lounging or napping on, it may be an issue, especially for people with sharp noses. Although some fabrics have a distinctive odor, others are fairly neutral smelling. Some natural fibers have inherent scent qualities, like silk and wool, while others get their odor from the types of dyes or finishes used. For the latter, laundering doesn't always get rid of a fabric's scent because the dye is impregnated in the fabric and the finishing processes also contribute to any aroma the fabric may have. So if you're worried that a particular fabric may be too strong smelling for your slipcover, get a sample, launder it, and check it. Sniff before you buy!

Particularly with slipcovers, you have to be sure the motif always runs the correct way across the entire sofa or chair. Our recommendation here and throughout this book is to use a small, all-over print fabric for creating slipcovers. It saves you time, money, and sewing frustration, and you'll be less prone to grow weary of your slipcover if you take this advice (see Chapters 2 and 6 for more on prints). You'll find that small, allover prints also impart a cozy, calming feeling; something about that random repetition is very lulling to the eye.

Many books, including the one you're currently reading, urge you to exercise restraint when you mix patterns. Two or three patterns are plenty. A room bustling with four or five different patterns can impart an unrestful and chaotic feeling. You can add visual interest with other elements, such as texture, rather than inundating the space with too many patterns (see the next section).

Making use of texture

Introducing texture is a great way to add a low-key sense of style. Not everyone likes a bold or diverse color palette. If you want to work in neutral colors but don't want it to get boring, look for fabrics with texture. Woven fabrics — such as damasks and twills — are wonderful for window treatments and slipcovers.

Fabrics with *nap* (in this case, fabrics made with raised threads that impart a fuzzy texture, and which "change" color when brushed one way or the other) — such as velvet, velveteen, and corduroy —are also good choices. Quilted fabric, like matelasse, is a nice choice for slipcovers and adds a bit of cushion for good measure. Faux-suedes add texture and are durable as well as washable.

You can also consider introducing a small bit of texture to the body of a conservative-looking creation: Add a pillow or skirt to a slipcover or a tieback or edging to a window treatment. A little can go a long way.

Uncovering Sources of Project-Planning Inspiration

Whenever you're planning a new project, you have a ton of items to keep straight. On top of all these elements, you also need to find design ideas. Where do you get the spark of inspiration? This section can provide some insight.

Catalogs and magazines

If you're like us, you get about a million home-design retail catalogs in the mail each month. Don't throw them away. They're a great place to find inspiration. Most of these companies also sell a nice array of drapery rods, poles, brackets, finials, and *holdbacks* (tiebacks made from hard materials). Take a look at the different styles to see which ones appeal to you. Some may give you a few ideas of your own, either to make (see Chapter 8), or to pick up cheap secondhand at resale stores, flea markets, or garage sales (see Chapter 4).

If you subscribe to *Architectural Digest* or a similar magazine, or if you receive any of the do-it-yourself design magazines — the market now has more than ever before — you're sure to find tons of ideas. If you can't swing a costly subscription, check out the library (your mom would surely approve of this idea).

The good ol' public library

Books on interior design, architecture, the history of fabric, and fine art books are all great idea sources, if you're fortunate enough to have your own library (Mark has an awe-inspiring one!). If you don't have one, remember that another ideal place to search for design ideas is waiting for you right in your hometown — the public library.

In this digital age, many people often forget how peaceful and edifying libraries can be. You can really concentrate and evaluate when you're surrounded by nothing but quiet. Make the time to "study" there, as you used to do as a kid, if only for an hour, to find your inspiration (and at the right price!).

Museums and historic homes

To get a feel for classical designs of the past, museums and historic homes pro-vide a wonderful opportunity for study and contemplation. On-site curators verify the historical accuracy and caretakers tend to the design elements of these places, allowing for a pleasant, informative visit. Meet these profession-als if you can and ask questions. Be sure to inquire as to whether photographs are prohibited before taking them.

To locate a historic home that is open to visitors, check out this helpful Web site: www.nationalregisterofhistoricplaces.com.

Open houses and house tours (also known as barging in on the neighbors)

When an important (or not so important) home is up for sale, the real estate office handling the sale arranges a no-invitation visitation time so prospective buyers can see the goods. These open houses are given to create local "buzz," and they usually last for a full weekend. They're another wonderful (and super fun) opportunity to get design info.

In a similar vein, some cities offer (for a nominal fee that usually goes to char-ity) tours of historic neighborhood homes, some of which have been lovingly restored to their original splendor. It's an opportunity for the homeowners to show off their restoration work, and for you to meet like-minded folks who love house history, and to contribute to a worthwhile cause. Some towns feature designer showcases of newly constructed homes or holiday-themed tours to raise money for a community project; these tours may also be a good resource.

If you have some drawing talent, make a sketch of the design detail you want to re-create at home. Yes, you can whip out your minicamera or cell phone to take pictures, but please be discreet — you're still in somebody's home!

TV and the Internet

TV design shows are rampant. Just turn on your TV (of course, we recommend the one Mark's on, *While You Were Out* on TLC) and see if they're doing any-thing you want to try. Write down the name and date of the episode, and later do an Internet search for that show's Web site, where you're sure to find infor-mation and additional links that can provide inspiration.

The Internet is also a great design resource. Just log on to the Web, type in the specific design topic — for example, "kitchen valance" — into a search engine, and happy hunting.

Fabric stores

Visiting a great fabric store with an amazing array of fabric is a wonderful way to start the process. Sure, we can explain to you what organza or damask or toile looks and feels like, but until you see it and touch it yourself, you can't decide if it's right for you and your needs. Believe us, the sales help won't look at you funny if you spend an hour at a fabric store and buy nothing. Getting educated about what you like and don't like about fabric is an important step in creating the projects in this book.

Some Assembly Required: Necessary Construction Skills

You have quite a few construction options for making window treatments and slipcovers. Whether you sew or not is up to you, as we offer a few sewing alternatives, such as using hot glue and iron-on bonding tape. You also need to measure with a measuring tape and drape fabric to get the look you're seeking.

Measuring makes it right

Measuring correctly is essential to making your creation the best it can be. Accurately determining your window's width and length and your furniture's width, length, and depth is the first step in determining your fabric needs.

Before you begin any project, take a look at our two measuring chapters, Chapters 6 and 10, for tips on figuring out how much fabric you need for your style of windows or furniture. You can also find some info there on cutting your fabric, making patterns, and calculating your seam allowances.

Folding, draping, tying, and more

Many of our simplest projects call for finessing and arranging fabric by way of folding, draping, tucking, and tying. In our easy window treatment chapter, Chapter 7, we talk about using folded throws, draped fabric to create swags that loop around a decorative rod, and adding clips to create fast and beautiful treatments. In our simple slipcover chapter, Chapter 11, we focus on tucking, pinning, tying, and draping fabric or even flat bed sheets for a great covering effect.

Although they may sound easy, these skills actually take a bit of practice to get the look you want, so don't feel discouraged if it takes you a few tries (or more).

After you achieve the look you love, you can add a bit of panache with knock-out accessories. (Check out Chapters 8 and 12 for adding accessories to your window treatments and slipcovers.)

Sewing (or gluing or bonding)

This book divides projects into three categories: easy no-sew or low-sew window treatments and slipcovers; intermediate-level projects that require some sewing knowledge but also offer a few sewing alternatives; and more complex projects where sewing with a machine is a must and some specific sewing knowledge is required.

Generally, the easier the project, the less reliant on a sewing machine you need to be. In some cases, you can substitute sewing with a hot glue gun, safety pins, or even Stitch Witchery or another brand of iron-on bonding tape. Check out the individual project chapters for specifics.

Here's a quick rundown on your sewing choices.

Sewing with a sewing machine

Sewing with a machine is the quickest and easiest way to construct a window treatment or slipcover. You'll be folding fabric to sew hems with our fold-and-fold method (see Chapter 14), sewing straight lines across fabric to create rod sleeves, joining two or even three panels of fabric together to get adequate width for your windows and furniture, and sewing fabric pieces together with simple seams.

A sewing machine is also helpful for sewing on accessories. Any sewing machine that can sew a straight stitch and a zigzag stitch works fine, and the ability to reverse to back tack is helpful, but not essential. If your sewing machine has a zipper foot attachment, you can use it for adding zippers to slipcover cushions (see Chapter 17).

Sewing by hand

A needle and thread come in handy when you only have to make a few stitches here and there, for low-sew window treatments, and for attaching buttons, bows, appliqués, and other accessories, especially delicate trims that your sewing machine could damage (see Chapters 8 and 12 for more on accessories and the best ways to apply them). Just remember: Have a few sizes of needles around for different fabric weights; the heavier the fabric, the thicker the needle.

Using a glue gun, bonding tape, and more

You also have a few other options besides a sewing machine or sewing by hand when working these projects. You can use

- ✔ A **glue gun** (a tool that melts a stick of glue and ejects it in a thin stream) bonds fabric to fabric for a long-lasting hold and is a great alternative to sewing, especially if you confine its use to an area that you can't see after the project is finished.

- ✔ **Iron-on bonding tape,** such as Stitch Witchery, which you use in conjunction with an iron and pressing cloth, can take the place of sewing hems at the bottom of your window treatment. You can also use it to attach accessories, like trims and appliqués. You place this tape between two layers of fabric and iron over the fabric. The iron's heat melts the tape and adheres the two pieces of fabric together.

- ✔ **Fray Check** is a sealant for fabric; it prevents nicks and edges from fraying.

- ✔ **Safety pins** are a terrific way to create no-sew window treatments (see some of the projects in Chapter 7), and they're also useful for securing slipcovers (see Chapter 12).

Check out Chapter 5 to discover more about these handy notions.

Creating a Workspace and Gathering Your Supplies

Organizing your workspace is an essential step in the creative process. Having everything you need at your fingertips allows you to work unimpeded and quickly, not to mention lowering the dreaded frustration level. Here's all you need to get it all together.

Your worktable

Did your mom or grandmother have a sewing room when you were growing up? Who wouldn't love a room of one's own, to dream, create, and indulge one's senses? If you don't have a room to set up a permanent workspace for your sewing projects, what can you do? Don't panic. You can use any large table, with just a bit of specification.

You need a large, flat surface on which to spread out, measure, pin, and cut fabric, and you need a stable spot for your sewing machine. Because sewing machines tend to shake, use a sturdy table, such as a strong kitchen or dining room table. If you're limited by space as to how large a table you have, set up an adjacent card table so you have room to spread out your fabric and so your fabric has a place to rest when coming out of the sewing machine, especially when you're sewing large fabric panels.

You also want to cover a smooth-surfaced table with a table pad or secured tablecloth to keep your fabric from sliding around. If you plan to do quite a bit of sewing and don't mind the extra work, consider covering your worktable with half-inch thick cotton batting, to add some nonsliding padding. Roll the batting out across the table and secure it by taping it under each corner of the worktable, or use extra-large rubber bands at the table edges to keep the batting in place.

If you're really limited for space, you may be tempted to try to work on the floor. We suggest you skip the floor because it's *really* hard on your body. But if you have a strong constitution and the floor is your *only* option, make sure you kneel on a pillow, or buy a gardener's foam pad. You'll be able to work longer, and your knees will surely thank you for it! And always tape a large clean sheet to the floor so your fabric doesn't pick up any dust, dirt, or dog or cat hair. We don't recommend working on a bed; it's too soft, and there's just too good a chance you'll cut through your bedspread or duvet.

If you're committed to setting up a permanent sewing space, you may want to invest in some sewing room furniture. Check out sewing centers, tables, and cabinets made especially for sewing rooms at www.joann.com.

Let there be light

Adequate light is an essential ingredient for any creative endeavor. If you can't set your worktable up near a source of natural light, get a floor lamp or other large light source with a full-spectrum light bulb so everything — from the pattern repeat to the selvage edge to the matching thread color — is crystal clear. Doing so also serves you well if the only time you get to work on your creation is in the evening.

Bags, baskets, boxes, and more

We understand but don't adhere to the "out of sight, out of mind" school of thought when it comes to sewing areas. Keeping everything hidden away may make for a peaceful-looking room, but we also firmly believe that the better you can actually see your trims, buttons, threads, and tools, the more inspired you'll be to create. And yes, you can keep all your sewing stuff in an old toolbox that tucks away in a closet, but finding what you want when you want it can be a nightmare.

Instead consider storing your supplies in clear shoeboxes or plastic containers with lids that pop open and plastic bags that zip closed. Clear, partitioned storage containers with lids, like the ones used to store and separate jewelry, are great for buttons, snaps, and other small notions. You don't have to sort your stuff more than once and aren't tricked into thinking you don't have enough of one thing to complete a project. You also save tons of time and money because you use up what you have at home and don't spend several trips running back and forth to the fabric store buying items you don't need. Store your fabric in boxes or baskets away from heat and light and label them well so you know just where everything goes. Gently fold and don't overstack your fabric so it doesn't permanently crease.

Nearer to thee (your references, that is)

Along with our supplies, we also like to keep our references handy, whether they're art books, color samples, or a bunch of photos we've torn out of magazines and stored in a file. We keep the loose items in a color notebook so they're always close at hand when we shop, and easy to locate when we're ready to begin a project. (See Chapter 2 for more about keeping a notebook.)

To keep everything in its place, add a small shelving unit with labels — it can save you a huge amount of time having everything you need within arm's reach. Just slide your basket or box of bobbins into the shelf labeled "bobbins" and you never have to dig around for them or crane your neck from shelf to shelf. Line the back of one shelf with pegboard and you have a great place to hang your scissors, ruler, and even your cloth measuring tape.

Iron and ironing board

You need your iron and ironing board close by your cutting table because you need to press seams open while you create. Ideally you can permanently set up your ironing board so you don't have to open and close it every time you use it. To keep your ironing accoutrements handy, get a hanging wire basket meant for fruit and attach it to any loop-like metal part on the underside of your ironing board. You can keep your pressing cloth, water spray bottle, and even your Stitch Witchery or other iron-on bonding tape right where you need it. If your workspace is limited, pick up a tabletop ironing board, but make sure it's wide and large enough to make your ironing job easier, not harder.

Chapter 2

Choosing the Right Fabric for the Job

*Y*ou need to consider many different factors when determining which fabric is right for your project. For instance, when choosing fabric for your bedroom window treatment, you need to determine whether you want it to darken the room or lighten it. On the other hand, if you need fabric to cover the family room sofa, you need to discover if it can withstand the test of time and the rigors of your washing machine — not to mention your kids and pets. Additionally, you must consider the big-three fabric senses: sight, smell, and touch (see Chapter 1). And last, but not least, you need to keep in mind the size of your pocketbook.

Selecting a fabric that meets all these qualifications may not always be easy, but it's possible. Just imagine the day you find the fabric with the right look, smell, and feel to match your project. Add to that accomplishment the fact that it's easy to care for, durable, and hey, look . . . it's on sale! In this chapter we show you what to look for when choosing fabrics, so that someday soon, that wonderful day will come.

Factoring in Fiber Content

One of the first things you need to consider when choosing fabrics is fiber content. *Fibers* are what provide the respective characteristics of how fabrics look, feel, and respond to environmental factors. Knowing a bit about how fibers are joined and how they're composed can help you make an informed decision about which fabrics may work for you.

Buying blends

Although you may prefer all-cotton fabric for your clothes, don't be a fiber snob with your drapery and curtains fabric. Natural and synthetic blends (for example, part-polyester/part-cotton fabrics) are terrific for window treatments. Not only are they durable, wrinkle-resistant, and easy to clean, but they also don't *pill* (when bits of fabric break away and turn into little balls along the surface of the fabric), they don't hold stains, and their price-per-yard is right on the money.

Types of fibers

Fibers are either *natural, synthetic* (either plant- or chemical-based), or a mix of the two, called *fiber blends.* These fibers are spun into *yarn,* which is in turn knit or woven into *fabric.*

Each type of fiber has its own unique traits:

✔ Natural fibers, such as cotton, silk, linen, or wool, feel soft to the touch, but often tend to wrinkle and shrink and need more ironing than synthetic materials. Natural fibers also tend to fade in color with repeated washing, because the colors are dyed in, not chemically sealed in the way they are with synthetics.

✔ Synthetic fibers (also called *man-made fibers*), such as polyester, nylon, acrylic, and microfibers, are durable and longwearing. The fabrics made from this type of fiber shed dirt better than natural-fiber fabrics. Best of all, they don't shrink.

✔ Blends, which contain both natural and synthetic fibers spun together, enable you to get the best qualities of both: dye fastness, durability, shape retention, longer wear, softness, and drapability.

The fiber effect

Fibers are to fabric what flour is to bread. They're the major ingredients that make up fabric. The kind of fiber that is used to make a fabric determines a number of factors, including:

✔ **Care:** The fiber you're considering determines whether your fabric is easily washable or needs to be dry-cleaned, and it determines whether it needs to be pressed, or ironed, after you launder it.

✔ **Durability:** This factor shows you how sturdy a fiber can make the fabric and determines whether the fabric is *colorfast* (the quality of holding color against the rigors of detergent and water), keeps its shape, and whether it rapidly fades when exposed to sunlight.

✔ **Texture (or feel):** Getting the texture right is more important for slipcovers than for window treatments. The texture can tell you whether the fabric feels soft enough to the touch and will be comfortable.

✔ **Weight:** This factor helps you determine whether your fabric is heavy enough to cover a sofa or lightweight enough for the type of window treatment you want.

Chronicling the life and times of fiber

Fibers are the basic material used to create fabric, and different types of fibers go in and out of fashion. Once upon a time, all clothing was made of natural fibers like cotton, linen, silk, or wool, depending on where you lived or how much money you had. In the 20th century, however, many fiber innovations came about, including

✔ **Rayon:** The first *cellulosic* (made of reconstituted wood pulp, or cellulose), or man-made, fiber to mimic silk, rayon was discovered in the 1920s.

✔ **Nylon:** An early synthetic fiber (made of polychemicals), sturdy nylon soon followed rayon in the late '30s.

✔ **Acrylic:** An easy-care alternative to wool, acrylic was big in the 1950s.

✔ **Polyester:** In the 1960s, for some, fashion was all about returning to the earth and all-natural fibers, but for others, space-age polyesters ruled.

✔ **Other synthetics:** Polyester and other synthetics continued to gain ground in the disco-bent '70s.

✔ **Stretch fabrics and microfibers:** Remember those spandex pants? They blossomed in the '80s, leading to another elaboration on the stretch-fabric theme: microfibers.

✔ **Ultramodern microfibers:** Ultrasuede is our favorite microfiber. Many microfiber innovations are common in the fabric scene today. Some of them have qualities that silk-lovers can only dream about. They're more durable, washable, and resistant to water stains.

Modern microfibers can be woven into any type of fabric, from heavy suede-like fabrics to faux silks. Sometimes they're so close to the real thing that you can't tell them apart. Today more than 90 percent of the fibers in the world's fabric marketplaces are synthetic.

Weighing Your Fabric Options

You can choose from three fabric weights (lightweight, mediumweight, and heavyweight), although we want to point out that fabric doesn't have any hard and fast rules regarding weight. The most important factor in determining fabric weight is how appropriate it is for the look you're after and how comfortable you are working with it.

When choosing a lightweight fabric, pick one that isn't too slippery or flimsy if you feel it may be difficult for you to sew accurately; similarly some heavyweight fabrics may be a challenge to negotiate for someone without much experience. We recommend buying a half yard before you commit to be sure the fabric looks great, gives you the right look, and is easy to handle.

Lightweight fabrics

Lightweight fabrics are terrific for window treatments. Lightweight fabrics

- ✔ Let in light, fresh air, and afford a less-obstructed view
- ✔ Allow you some design variety
- ✔ Give a breezy feel and a sense of movement to a room
- ✔ Are usually easy to handle and move through your sewing machine

   For example, you can choose a lightweight fabric for one treatment and add it to another treatment for a layering effect. Silky, lightweight fabric is great for creating *swags* (the top part of a window treatment of the same name that drapes over the top of your window) and *cascades* (the part of the swag treatment that descends along the sides of the window frame). You may also want to consider lighter fabric for casement curtains and curtains with ruffles.

If treated gently, window treatments made from lightweight fabric can last as long as medium- or heavyweight fabrics (see the next two sections on medium- and heavyweight fabrics), though they may not stand up as well against the onslaught of kids or pets. If your home is blessed with sticky paws and hands that have a tendency to yank or scratch, keep them in mind when shopping for your fabric.

Although lightweight fabrics work well with window treatments, they're really not suitable for slipcovers. They can't withstand the force of the human body, and most lightweight fabrics are on the sheer or semisheer side and don't provide enough coverage to keep your sofa's old fabric from peeking through.

However, if you want to be a design rebel, you may try lightweight fabrics as a slipcover for less-used furniture. If you love the look of a delicate slipcover fabric for an airy, ethereal effect, and you plan to apply it to a bedroom settee where you mostly lay out your clothes (certainly never doing the full-on couch potato routine), why not consider a lightweight fabric? Take a swatch or even a half yard of the lightweight fabric home and see how you like the effect. Test the fabric to see how easy it is to sew a hem, how the fabric handles in your machine, and if the fabric is substantial enough to hold a sewn hem and not too delicate and slippery so that it slides off your settee.

Some of the more popular lightweight fabrics include

- ✔ **Batiste:** This sheer, soft, plain-weave fabric is usually made of cotton or a cotton/poly blend and often features lengthwise streaks because of the type of yarn used to make it. It's a nice fabric for constructing sheer window treatments, and the blend version launders especially well. Batiste is a simple, inexpensive fabric that works well on a bathroom or kitchen window treatment, which you can further embellish with a light trim.

- ✔ **Challis**: This soft, plain-weave fabric usually comprises cotton, rayon, wool, or a blend of any of these three fibers. Challis is ideal for window treatments because it offers a good drape and comes in many prints. Challis also works well for any kind of swag treatment. It blocks light well, though not totally, but you can add a lining to make it more effective. It's a moderately expensive fabric.

- ✔ **Charmeuse:** This soft, woven satin/crepe fabric has an excellent drape, which makes it perfect for many types of window treatments. We love charmeuse for an elegant feel for bedrooms. Its face is lustrous, and its back is dull; you can use whichever side appeals to you. It's a moderately expensive fabric.

- ✔ **Chiffon:** This very lightweight, inexpensive, sheer, plain-weave fabric has a nonshiny finish and excellent drape, making it another classic window treatment fabric to consider. It was once made exclusively of silk, but now is available in polyester and other synthetic forms. It launders well and, like batiste, is a good choice for a room where you want a lot of light, such as a bathroom or kitchen. It also makes for a lovely swag, or swag and cascade.

- ✔ **Crepe:** This fabric has an all-over crinkly, pebbly, or puckered texture, the result of a traditional crepe-weaving technique, embossing, or a chemical treatment. The textured surface can add character to a simple window treatment. It's a moderately expensive fabric.

- ✔ **Eyelet:** This fabric features small cutout decorative areas surrounded by stitching. It's an appropriate fabric for many types of curtains. A beautiful type of eyelet to consider for a cafe curtain is broderie anglaise, which is an embroidered cotton fabric with a pierced eyelet design. Eyelets are usually all cotton and thus have a tendency to shrink. Pretreat them according to Chapter 3 and wash them in cold water, or look for one blended with a synthetic for easier care. Eyelet is a moderately expensive fabric.

✔ **Gauze, mesh, and fishnet:** What open-weave fabrics, such as gauze, mesh, and fishnet, lack in fiber content they make up with for with high style and low cost. They add texture and visual interest to windows while allowing in light. We love these fabrics for country and beach houses, where a nautical motif is ideal and privacy is less of an issue. Remember to keep your treatment panels simple and let the fabric be the star.

When choosing an open-weave fabric for a floor-length window treatment, hang your fabric over a rod or pole for a while, so that the loose fibers have a chance to stretch out. Doing so prevents the fabrics from having a pooling effect later, because these fabrics have a tendency to droop and hang a bit lower than more tightly woven fabrics.

✔ **Lace:** Lace is light and always a nice, feminine addition to a bedroom, powder room, or even a kitchen. Try lace draperies or curtains in rooms that feature antiques and Victorian-era furniture. Lace ruffle curtains are always adorable for a girl's room. The prices for lace vary considerably. Polyester lace is the least expensive, blended lace is a bit more, and cotton lace can range from expensive to very expensive.

Polyester lace is easiest to launder and work with, but poly-cotton blends and all-cotton lace also are available in many widths (for more about lace, see Chapter 7).

✔ **Organza:** A thin, plain-weave, sheer fabric sometimes made of silk and sometimes made of synthetics, such as nylon and polyester, organza is often used for wedding dresses, but it also makes a terrific fabric for light window treatments. Its applications are similar to batiste or chiffon, but its texture is somewhat stiffer. It's a moderately expensive fabric to buy.

When working with sheer fabrics, more often is more. Unless you're seeking a streamlined, ultramodern sheer treatment, be sure to add two to three times the measured width so you have adequate fullness and coverage in your sheer-fabric treatment. Otherwise, your final product may appear a bit flimsy.

✔ **Plissé:** This fabric is usually made from rayon or cotton, and features a bumpy or blistered effect (made by applying a caustic soda). It comes in solids and prints and can be semisheer or opaque. Some plissé loses its texture when washed, so be sure to test a swatch before pretreating your fabric. It's moderately expensive.

✔ **Voile:** This fabric comes in smooth and crinkly versions with a plain-weave and a crisp finish. Voile is most commonly made of cotton, but also comes in silk, rayon, acetate, and wool versions. Some voiles are printed, some are solid, and most are semisheer. Consider it for a hallway or foyer curtain. It's a perfect fabric for bathroom curtains or any spot where a sheer or light application with a bit of firmness for staying power (against steam or heat, for example) is appropriate. It's moderately expensive.

Mediumweight fabrics

Most decorator fabrics fall into the category of mediumweight and heavy-weight. Mediumweight fabrics are the gold standard for both window treatments and slipcovers. You can find the most variety of fabrics in the mediumweight category, so your choices will be very wide-ranging. When making window treatments, mediumweight fabrics

✔ Provide privacy

✔ Block light when used for simple window panels

✔ Have the weight you'll need to create treatments with pleats or valances

You can use mediumweight fabric to make swags, as long as the fabric drapes well. Roll the bolt out to check.

Mediumweights also hold up well for most slipcovers. When making slipcovers, mediumweight fabrics

✔ Work for dining room tables, ottomans, washing machine covers, and other slipcover projects that need a strong fabric, but don't necessarily need heavyweight fabric

✔ Don't work if the sofa, armchair, or loveseat you're covering will be treated roughly

Some examples of mediumweight fabric include

✔ **Brocade:** The queen of slipcover fabrics, brocades once were made exclusively from silk and were a favorite of the very rich. Now, however, they're made from more affordable synthetics and blends. Brocade is a two-toned Jacquard fabric, due to its satin-and-twill weave, and comes in many colors and many motifs. It's a moderately inexpensive to expensive fabric.

Brocades come in many weights that are appropriate for window treatments, from lightweight for creating flowing draperies, to medium- and heavyweights for making London and Roman shades. Care for your brocade creations according to its fiber content.

Brocade's raised design gives a formal, opulent look perfect for living and dining rooms. Brocade is popular for slipcover use because of its heavier feel and also because its slightly raised texture and color variation hides dirt. Some brocades acquire a whole new (softer and drapier) appearance when washed. It may be worth testing a sample if you think you want this effect for a window treatment that requires drapability.

✔ **Brocatelle:** This silk-and-linen–weave Jacquard fabric is similar to brocade but has a slightly different look. It features a raised design, which is formed by a satin-and-twill weave, and originally was created to mimic tooled leather. Like brocade fabric, brocatelle lends a luxurious, formal tone, comes in a few weights, and is ideal to use for both window treatments where you want a bit of coverage and slipcovers. Like its cousin brocade, brocatelle is a moderately inexpensive to expensive fabric.

- ✔ **Chenille:** This fuzzy-pile, velvety fabric is made from a caterpillarlike yarn. It's best used for draped and pinned slipcovers. Chenille gives a cushy, warming feeling to any room, so it's nice for dens and family rooms. Your wee ones will especially love to sit on a chair covered with the "little caterpillar" fabric. A kilim-style chenille, which is flatter and features intricate designs, is also available. Most types of chenille fabric are expensive.

- ✔ **Chintz:** This fabric takes its name from the Indian word *chint,* meaning "broad, gaudily printed fabric." Chintz was a popular decorating fabric in the 1940s, '50s, and '60s, and it's back in fashion today. A plain-weave fabric with a neutral background and a bright floral print, chintz is usually made of cotton or a cotton-blend.

Some chintz has a shiny finish, achieved with a glaze, which is quite durable and repels dust. However it can lose its shiny finish when washed. Dry-clean this type of chintz to retain its shine.

The unglazed, nonshiny chintz is called *cretonne.* Some people prefer the nonshiny type for slipcovers and the shiny type for draperies; it's totally a matter of taste. Either finish-type chintz is a lovely choice for window treatments or slipcovers, and is moderately inexpensive.

- ✔ **Corduroy:** A cotton or blended fabric part of the velvet family, corduroy is a pile fabric that features medium-to-wide, three-dimensional vertical-cut piles called *wales.* It has a soft luster and is very comfortable to touch, yet it's very strong and durable, making it a natural for slipcovers. Another bonus to corduroy: it's inexpensive.

Choosing corduroy adds texture, warmth, and depth to your decor. We love corduroy slipcovers and curtains or draperies in a family room or den.

- ✔ **Cotton:** Cotton is versatile, affordable, and easy to sew. It provides moderate to full coverage, and comes in the widest range of patterns and prints.

If you hate to iron, consider a different fabric instead of cotton. All-cotton fabrics need to be pressed after you launder them.

You can't beat using kerchief/bandanna fabric, gingham, and other printed cottons for creating *valances* (a top-only window treatment) and curtains. These simple cotton prints bring to mind the decor of the past when fabrics were known for their simplicity.

For treatments that call for an informal fabric, such as curtains or draperies with tab tops (see Chapter 16), printed cotton is a perfect match. What could be cuter than a gingham valance over a sunny kitchen window (see Chapter 15)? A set of cafe curtains in an informal printed cotton is another kitchen classic (see Chapter 15). Polka dot–printed fabric is especially nice for a little girl's room. Bandanna-printed fabric adds a nice Western touch to your little cowboy's room, and darker cotton prints and plaids are great in an older boy's room, in studies, and in family rooms. Cotton fabrics are also woven with embellishments. For a more formal treatment, consider dotted Swiss or claret cotton with contrasting woven dots.

Formal-looking cotton prints also are available for rooms that require more drama. These prints tend to be dyed deeper colors and feature ornate motifs. We love blue-and-white floral prints for a swag and cascade treatment (see Chapter 16) in a dining room. Chintz (see earlier item in this list) is a more formal cotton-print fabric nice for draperies and curtains, and its tighter weave keeps light out.

✔ **Damask:** Originally made from silk (in Damascus, hence its name) damask is a mediumweight cotton or cotton-synthetic blend fabric that is similar to brocade. Damasks are woven on a Jacquard loom in one color and many have a formal feeling owing to their ornate, large floral patterns, animal patterns, or Renaissance-era motifs. Damask is also available in informal and geometric patterns. When damask weaves are multicolored, they're called *lampas.* The range of damask fabrics tends to be moderate to expensive.

Two important benefits with damask are

- It's reversible, so you can choose one fabric and use both sides for a contrasting effect.

- Like brocade, it hides dirt.

✔ **Hand-stitched and embroidered fabric:** Always a good choice when coupled with a simple curtain or drapery design, hand-stitched or embroidered fabrics are beautiful and really shine through when nothing distracts the eye. Crewel-worked, cotton-blend fabrics tend to be easy to work with.

Crewel is a type of embroidery that uses a wool yarn for a highly raised effect. Crewel comes in a variety of colorful motifs, usually the floral and vine designs based on the East Indian tree of life designs and their British interpretation. The fabric upon which the crewel is added tends to be applied to opaque cotton or linen blends that are quite sturdy and block light well, so crewel-worked fabric is a nice choice for window treatments. Try it with a simple curtain panel so nothing distracts from this beautiful multicolored embroidery. Crewel-worked fabrics from India tend to be moderately inexpensive to expensive, and most hand-stitched or embroidered fabric is expensive.

Crewel usually has to be dry-cleaned, so keep this in mind if you don't like trips to the drycleaners.

✔ **Jacquard:** J.M. Jacquard invented these types of loomed fabrics, which include brocades, brocatelles, damasks, and tapestries. All Jacquard fabrics feature a complicated pattern woven into the fabric as part of its structure. The loom on which Jacquards are made controls each yarn separately, raising it or lowering it to create its unique design and texture. Jacquards work beautifully with most window treatments. They're especially great with formal sophisticated juxtapositions of treatments like valances and pleats. Jacquards are moderately inexpensive to expensive.

✔ **Linen:** Linen is a type of fabric woven entirely from linen yarns, which are made from flax fibers. Many linen fabrics have a loosely woven texture that allows in light and air when used on windows, yet it's a strong, durable fabric. More tightly woven linens that block more light are available. However, many types of linen are a bit scratchy, so if you're considering one for a slipcover, make sure you like its texture. If you want to use linen for a slipcover, look for blended versions that wear well; a blend also cuts down on your ironing time. Linen is moderately expensive.

You can also find faux linen on the market, which is less expensive and easier to care for. Don't forget that 100-percent linen needs to be ironed after laundering and creases easily.

✔ **Matelasse:** This cotton or cotton-blend, double-woven fabric, usually woven on a Jacquard loom, has the appearance of being quilted or padded. This fabric works well as a slipcover fabric for furniture to which you want to add a bit of softness, or a padded effect. It has a tiny bit of stretch to it, so if your measurements aren't perfect, it's forgiving. Matelasses are moderately expensive.

✔ **Satin:** Satins come in many forms (natural, synthetic, and blends), and they're woven to create a smooth, lustrous surface. Upholstery satin (a heavier weight than satins used for clothing) is appropriate for slipcovers.

Satins and sateens make wonderful draperies and curtains. Satin's finish is shiny, while sateen's is somewhat duller. Their beautiful texture adds a touch of luster and glamour to any room. When choosing this type of fabric for its draping quality, be sure to unfurl the bolt quite a few yards and test it well, because not all satins and sateens drape well (see Chapter 7 for a discussion on drapability). Synthetic and blended satins tend to be moderately expensive, while natural satins can cost more.

✔ **Silk:** Draperies made from silks look fabulous, and we're equally enamored by unfinished silks, such as doupioni and shantung, that feature gorgeous, shiny finishes with natural nubs that give them texture. Regardless of your preference in finishes, all these silks drape beautifully.

Many medium- to heavyweight silks are available for use in draperies; however, using silk has three drawbacks:

- It's costly.

- Water can easily damage it (watch those spotting raindrops!).

- It tends to degrade when exposed to the sun more quickly than other fabrics.

You may want to consider lining silk to protect it from sun and water damage so that it lasts longer.

Many silks come in synthetic versions. Four nice alternatives to silk are rayon, cotton-rayon blends, viscose, and acetate. They all

- Mimic silk's unique (silky) texture that is perfect for drapery treatments

- Cost much less

- Hold up better and are less prone to sun and water damage — so your creation should last longer

✔ **Taffeta:** This plain-weave, tightly woven fabric is made from silk or synthetics and has a smooth, crisp texture, making it a good choice for draperies. Silk taffeta is moderately expensive in price and is smooth and shiny on both sides, making it a natural for window treatments that tie back to expose their underside. It comes in a variety of truly gorgeous prints and colors, and the polyester versions are very well priced. Because taffeta is shiny, it reflects light, making the room seem larger and brighter. Keep this pretty fabric in mind for small rooms you want to appear bigger than they really are.

✔ **Toile:** A cotton fabric printed with one-color depictions of 18th- and 19th-century life, toile is similar to chintz, but it's unglazed, so it doesn't have the same shiny finish. *Toile de Jouy* (a town in France) features historic scenes of (especially) French country life; federal toile features scenes from 19th-century America, and toile de Indy shows historic East Indian scenes. Chinese and Rococo toiles also are available. Most toiles are moderately expensive.

✔ **Ultrasuede (and other synthetic microfiber faux-suedes):** Ultrasuede is a durable and flexible fake suede fabric that is much easier to sew than the real thing. Use the heavyweight type for slipcovers. Adding a Teflon sewing-machine foot when sewing Ultrasuede can be helpful (see Chapter 4). Ultrasuede is the most recognizable brand of this type of synthetic suede, and it tends to be expensive; less expensive versions are available, if you find Ultrasuede's price prohibitive.

Choose mediumweight Ultrasuede (and other synthetic microfiber faux-suedes) to mimic real suede at half the price and hassle. Ultrasuede curtains are perfect for studies, dens, and men's offices, because they add a masculine touch.

Heavyweight fabrics

Heavyweight fabrics add great window coverage. You can use them with many of the window treatment or especially the sofa slipcover projects in this book.

Heavyweight fabric in window treatments provides

- ✔ Superb light blockage, for those days when you want to sleep late
- ✔ A great way to keep in heat during the long winter months
- ✔ Durability against potentially destructive paws and little hands

Heavyweight fabric is also appropriate for slipcovers, especially those that get a lot of day-to-day use, such as family room sofas and chairs. When making slipcovers, heavyweights can

- ✔ Provide durability

    If you're covering a piece of furniture that gets used and battered, and you feel your sewing skills are good enough to handle a heavier fabric, when in doubt, go heavier!

- ✔ Spot-clean and launder well

Heavyweight fabrics are also wonderful for constructing some of the shade projects in Chapter 16.

Some popular heavyweight fabrics include

- ✔ **Canvas:** This multiuse medium- to heavyweight fabric is made from cotton and comes in a number of colors and prints. Canvases sometimes come with brushed finishes, too.

    Fabrics, such as canvas, sailcloth, and denim, in light- or mediumweights, can be a good choice for informal rooms that get a lot of wear and tear, such as rec rooms, dens, playrooms, or children's bedrooms. Dark, solid versions add a masculine touch to offices and men's spaces while keeping light out when used for window treatments. They're sturdy and launder easily. Canvases are priced inexpensively, though some printed canvas is moderately expensive.

    If you're seeking a fabric for an everyday slipcover that is strong and firm with a tight weave that repels liquids, is made of cotton, and is easy to launder, consider a durable canvas in a pretty color. Check the feel of the canvas by running your hand over it to make sure you're picking out a version that is durable but still soft enough to lounge upon.

- ✔ **Denim:** This inexpensive to moderately expensive twill fabric is made from cotton or cotton blends, and it's terrific — one of the sturdiest, long-lived, and practical fabrics. You probably know the navy-colored version as jeans fabric, but it's also available in other colors, such as white or off-white, which is called *drill.* Denim washes well and becomes softer over time. Look for denim with a bit of Lycra added for the stretch that helps make a great slipcover fit.

Plain cotton twills, such as canvas, sailcloth, and denim, in mediumweight fabrics, can be a good choice for informal rooms that receive considerable wear and tear, such as rec rooms, dens, playrooms, or children's bedrooms. Likewise, dark, solid twill fabrics add a masculine touch to offices and men's spaces. Printed denim is also available. You can find denim in many styles, including embroidered, and even Jacquard-woven denims, which combine the formal and informal in one fabric.

✔ **Duck:** A heavyweight cotton fabric that resembles canvas, duck comes in many colors and a few different weights, and it effectively blocks light. Just don't expect any quacking when you use this cotton fabric. It's ideal for making shades that require a stiff, sturdy fabric, like Roman and London shades. Duck is also a good choice for many of the no-sew curtains in Chapter 7, as an alternative to Ultrasuede or other faux-suede fabrics. Duck comes in solids, stripes, patterns, as well as a number of weights. A beautiful duck fabric can be the basis for a sophisticated bedroom treatment because you can add trims to embellish a plain duck. Another bonus to duck: It's inexpensive.

✔ **Novelty fabrics:** Vinyl (sometimes called faux leather or pleather), faux-suede, faux-fur, and other alternative fabrics are the way to go for fun, funky treatments. Faux-fur is either knit or woven in acrylic or modacrylic to create the fuzzy feel of an animal's fur. Faux-leathers are usually made of polyurethane laminate. Vinyls and faux-furs are thicker than regular fabrics and thus are harder to sew. Keep your treatment simple when using them for the first time (or consider using a glue gun; see Chapters 4 and 7 for more). Most novelty fabrics are inexpensive or moderately expensive.

Children and teenagers usually love novelty fabrics for their bedrooms, so keep them in mind when treating your kids' rooms.

✔ **Tapestries:** These multicolored, closely woven scenes-on-fabric — some modern, some reminiscent of medieval art or nature — are a perfect choice for smaller projects like ottomans and vanity stools. Because tapestries often can be heavier than even heavyweight fabric (and more expensive), keep sewing to a minimum and use heavyweight sewing machine needles.

✔ **Velvet:** Made from natural or man-made fibers, this soft yet tough fabric comes in a special upholstery version that features a sturdy backing and a deeper, thicker pile than the regular velvet that's used for making clothes.

Velvet suits any semiformal or formal window treatment, and it's perfect for re-creating a Victorian or turn-of-the-20th-century look. It's a natural for making rooms of any period with dark wood look extravagant and expensive. For example, try velvet draperies for dressing up doorways. Velvet draperies in the bedroom say "va-va-voom" like no other fabric.

Many weights of velvet are available; chose according to how much coverage and light blockage you require. Nylon velvet is a good choice for window treatments because of its excellent texture and durability. Most velvet is moderately expensive and some is expensive.

✔ **Velveteen:** Closer to corduroy than velvet, velveteen is woven with a shorter pile than velvet, and it's generally made only of cotton. It has a durable finish and comes in solids and prints. Look for one with twill backing, because it holds up better with slipcovers. Most velveteen is moderately expensive, but you can find some expensive versions.

Velvet, velveteen, and other textured or matte fabrics absorb light, making a room treated with them appear "closer" and smaller than it really is. Keep them in mind when treating an overlarge room you want to have a cozier feeling.

Keeping style in mind when choosing fabrics

Many tried-and-true, timeless styles are available, from the simple to the baroque, and many of them even look wonderful when mixed together in varying types of window treatments and slipcovers. In the following sections, we give you general descriptions of a few of our favorite styles.

Glamour

When you hear the word "glamour," many people think of 1930s film stars like Jean Harlow and Norma Shearer in overdone, fussy Hollywood mansions. However, a glamorous style can also be contemporary. Glamour is just another way of saying *luxurious*, which means using a combination of rich-looking, well-draping fabrics with cascading, fringed trims for draperies, and highly tactile fabrics like chenille and velvets/velveteens for slipcovers.

Another hallmark of this style is decorating all in one color, or one tone, for example, in all white or cream, or all-neutral tones. It gives the room a serene, almost floating, movie set-like feeling. If you don't like the feel of white or neutrals, another alternative is a muted color palette — rose-toned pinks instead of hot pinks, for example. To achieve this look, consider lustrous fabrics like taffeta and satins for window treatments and Jacquard-loomed fabrics like brocades, tapestries, and damasks for both window treatments and slipcovers. Damasks are especially suited for this style because they're all one color, though all Jacquards are well suited for slipcovers for bedroom furniture, such as a settee or loveseat.

The look of a chenille slipcover for a bedroom chair or chaise exudes glamour and works well not only in bedrooms, but also in dens, libraries, and even in living rooms.

Consider adding to your windows any of the valance projects in Chapter 15 or the double swag draperies in Chapter 16. You can also try any of the throw-type, no-sew slipcover projects in Chapter 12 to achieve an easy yet abundant, glamorous effect. Simple panels and tiebacks embellished with beaded trims, as well as swags and cascades with sheers underneath, are great glamour looks that never go out of style.

Ethnic

Ethnic is a general term for styles that originate in other countries, such as India, Mexico, Morocco, and others. Although generally not thought of in those terms, English country style, indeed, is an ethnic style, as is French country style. (Chintzes and toiles are, respectively, typical fabrics used in those two styles.)

You can easily bring a touch of the following countries into your home by way of their hallmark fabrics. These nations are famous either for their woven textiles, their hand-dyed silks, or their lace. Not all fabric stores carry ethnic fabrics. Check the phonebook for importers in your area, and call them to see if they stock fabrics. You can also search online for specific fabrics and order them through a reputable Internet source. Some ethnic fabrics are expensive because they're hand worked, but some are a bargain.

- ✔ **Africa:** You can add a definite African ethnic touch with intricately woven fabrics like kuba and kente cloth. These fabrics are truly beautiful and are still available at a comparatively low cost.

- ✔ **Central America:** The fabrics emblematic of this region are beautiful, intricately colored cotton weaves that are hand woven in the Mayan style, which employs a back-strap loom. They come in a variety of styles, such as huipiles (used for blouses), cintas (used for sashes), tzutes (used for carrying cloths), and perrajes (for shawls). These fabrics from Guatemala and Honduras are gaining popularity and tend to be a great value.

- ✔ **Far East:** Silks that feature traditional, ancient motifs of the Far East (buddhas, pagodas, pictograms) bring China, Japan, and Tibet instantly to mind. If silk is too expensive, look for comparable blends or synthetics.

- ✔ **India:** India is a textile mecca and nearly all the fabric imported from India is well worth exploring. You can find gorgeous fabric that is a great value.

- ✔ **Indonesia:** Some other typical ethnic fabrics are Indonesian ikat, batik, kilim-style chenille, and brocades.

- ✔ **Spain and Italy:** Ultrasuede and other synthetic suedes mimic the look and feel of real suede and bring to mind the rich-toned decors of Spain and Italy.

You can add ethnic looks in virtually any room, and you can even incorporate more than one such ethnic style into one room. For example, the hallmarks of traditional Mexican decor — ceramic tile, bright colors, rough-hewn woods, and wrought iron — look great with elements of rustic Italian decor, which are quite similar in feel.

You don't have to go overboard with ethnic fabrics to pack a real style punch. The following are just a few suggestions to help you include some ethnic flair in any room:

✔ Add a basic dining room chair slipcover made from a polyester-silk blend fabric with an Asian motif to an otherwise neutral room, and you have a beautiful focal point upon which to base Far Eastern decor.

✔ Mount a rod at ceiling height and allow your fabric to drape in a way to accentuate a room's architecture. Rooms with dormer windows or unusual shapes are great for expressing an ethnic feel. Try draping fabric in doorways to create an ethnic look, or for creating classic Oriental room elements, like ogees.

Any simple panel made from an ethnic fabric adds style to a room. Try the fray-bottom draperies for an exotic feel or the cafe curtains to bring to mind French country life, both from Chapter 15. Customize the simple Ultrasuede panel curtains in Chapter 7 with special cutouts.

✔ Cover an ottoman in a remnant or smaller piece of unique, ethnic fabric to add an ethnic tone.

✔ Embellish window treatments and slipcovers with colorful trims and tassels. Doing so brings to mind the bright color palettes of Mexico, India, and other countries; seek out types that echo typical styles of the region you're referencing.

When creating larger slipcovers with an ethnic look, seek out one special decorative element, such as trim or fringe, that is a hallmark of one ethnic style, and add it to a neutral-colored slipcover. Not only does the neutral color allow the decorative element to take center stage, but also when you redecorate or change your room's theme, you can just change the trim for a brand-new look. Check out Chapter 8, where we talk about alternative tieback ideas, and Chapter 13 for slipcover accessory ideas.

Vintage

The Edwardian, Regency, and Victorian periods are vintage styles, too, but in this section we're talking specifically about the period of American style from the 1930s to the 1950s. Emblematic of vintage style are simple cotton fabrics that were the standard bearers before wash-and-wear cotton-polyester blends made ironing a thing of the past for women in the workforce in the 1960s and 1970s. Vintage styles hearken back to an era when Mom was in the kitchen and the home was a female-engineered haven, with feminine-detailed fabric to match.

You can easily create vintage style by buying actual vintage fabrics (although it's increasingly more difficult to find fabric of this era in pristine condition and it tends to be quite costly) or reproductions (see Chapter 20 for sources). Many of the vintage-look fabrics used for slipcovers are called *bark cloth,* which usually is a durable cotton twill or blend with a slightly raised, barklike texture that features Western, fruit, tree/leaf, or Hawaiian or other tropical motifs. Some bark cloths that are dyed and not heavily embossed drape well, so you can consider them for panels in a window treatment.

Another hallmark of vintage styles are the silks and silk blends that once were referred to as Oriental silks, because they featured traditional or pastoral Asian scenes or motifs. Printed cottons that feature mid-century designs are a nice choice for window treatments, as is gingham; all were popular in mid-20th century America. Lace and kerchief fabrics used as trims lend a vintage flair, too. These cotton fabrics require a bit of ironing, especially after laundering, but they're truly charming. Another classic vintage-looking trim to consider adding is rickrack.

You can apply the vintage touch to any room, but boxy, square rooms look especially great when you add the softening effect that's emblematic of this style and look. Cotton blends with sweet prints are great for slipcovers in a child's bedroom. Bark cloth slipcovers work well in dens, sitting rooms, studies, living rooms, and bedrooms. The choice is yours, because they come in so many colors and patterns.

You can take nearly every project in this book and give it a vintage look simply by using a fabric that gives a 1940s or 1950s feel. A few projects to try to get that old-time feel include the lace shelf valance with ruffle (Chapter 7), ruffle-top curtains (Chapter 14), crisscross curtains (Chapter 14), the dining room table slipcover (Chapter 17), and, of course, the washing machine slipcover (Chapter 16).

Crafty

Crafty is the term we use to convey handmade quality. Crocheted, knitted, embroidered, and other hand-stitched fabrics, with plenty of cute detailing, are the essence of this style. Some simple (and less expensive) crewel-worked fabrics also provide a nice crafty touch, as do fabrics that feature cross-stitched borders and motifs and stencil work that mimics embroidery. You can create a truly one-of-a-kind look whenever you use fabric that has been embroidered to match a prevailing motif in your room.

Embroidery is a fantastic way to create that adorable, crafty style that's so popular these days. Your machine may have embroidery capabilities; if not, check out Chapter 20, where we recommend a source for buying iron-on transfer patterns for adding embroidery.

Crafty style is great for kitchens, dens, and kids' rooms, but you can always try it in your home office to offset the "all-work, no-play" style. You usually find most hand-embroidered fabric in smaller quantities so it's best applied to smaller slipcover projects, such as an ottoman or a vanity stool (but if you can find enough fabric yardage to cover a whole loveseat, then go for it). Try a large knitted or crocheted throw to cover an armchair; see Chapter 12. For windows, consider crotched fabric for simple swags, like the ones in Chapter 15. And the Contac paper shade project in Chapter 7 is a fun and crafty no-sew project that is fun to do with younger family members.

Americana

Sometimes called *traditional,* sometimes called *country,* sometimes called *colonial,* Americana is a classic look that employs all things down home — comfy, traditional, and . . . well, American (to decorators in European countries, Americana is an ethnic style!).

Although great for window treatments and slipcovers in virtually any room, Americana works especially well in kitchens, dining rooms, dens, and family rooms or living rooms because of the comfortable feeling it imparts. A tried-and-true style, it features the use of patchwork fabric, corduroy, flannel, denim, gingham, and sometimes-busy prints like chintz or toile. Its typical use of the red-white-and-blue color scheme can be refreshing when done in new, unexpected ways. This style really complements oak wood furniture or wood-paneled rooms.

Try the pleated sofa skirt slipcover project in Chapter 17 for a traditional all-American look. Trim it with an ornamental braid or ribbon. Cover an ottoman in a red, white, and blue fabric or one that features American images, for example, of the bald eagle or an antique scarf that features a state (you know the kind, with capitol, state flower, and state bird noted). For an interesting informal window treatment, make simple panels with American flag fabric (or you may even want to use the real thing) and attach them to a wooden rod with matching wooden rings. For a more formal room, try an arched valance made with a printed fabric, like a toile that features scenes from colonial-period life.

Some people are tempted to use another comfortable fabric, jersey (which is a flat, single-knit fabric), to achieve an all-American style; however, this fabric tends to stretch a bit and gives when used in making slipcovers. As a result, your creation doesn't hold its shape, so avoid using it. Instead, look for denim or twill with a small percentage of Lycra or other stretch fabric blended in with the cotton.

Modern

Some call it contemporary and some call it 21st century. No matter what you call it, modern style is a way of decorating that says "now," with touches of classic design elements of the past — specifically mid-century Danish and

American design — thrown in for good measure. Hallmarks of this style are furniture in light woods in straight or streamlined designs, bold, graphic fabric with geometric or modified atomic-age motifs (boomerangs and exploding atoms are the most common ones), and the use of mid-century tones, such as the combination of medium-light blue, bright orange, gray, and white. Modern always is streamlined, light, and elegant. It's sometimes minimalist, but it still has touches of design whimsy through use of color. Modern always features a total absence of flounce: no "extra" fabric or baroque embellishment.

Because it lacks froufrou, this style is ideal for men's hangouts, such as dens and libraries, as well as living rooms and boys' bedrooms.

Vinyl, Ultrasuede, and other synthetic leathers are hallmarks of the modern look. In their present incarnations, these fabrics never have been better constructed nor have they ever been easier to work with. They come in really terrific colors, too. Although they can take a bit longer to sew, their knockout effect is worth the extra effort.

Try vinyl to cover a stool or ottoman, and Ultrasuede (or any other microfiber that mimics suede) to create a basic slipcover for a chair or sofa. Making the car wash curtains in Chapter 7 is a great way to add fabric without a lot of flounce: The fabric hangs down and brings to mind mod 1960s design. Try it on windows or in doorways. For example, a Roman shade in a simple cotton duck is a streamlined and effective way to keep light out.

Examining Window Fabric Essentials

You have tons to think about when deciding on fabric for window treatments. Choosing the correct weight, texture, light-blocking or light-exposing qualities, and the fabric's durability are just the beginning. You also want it to look fantastic, don't you? In this section we discuss these qualities and cover a few applications so you can make the treatment you need and love.

Considering window fabric details

Wrap your head around these concepts for a few minutes before deciding on your fabric. If you spend some time considering your options now, when it comes time to look at dozens of fabrics at the store, you'll have a clearer idea of what will work best for your specific needs.

- ✔ **Durability:** This issue is important when considering fabrics for window treatments. Over time the sun can damage all fabrics, but silks are especially prone to sun rot. Consider lining silks to prolong their life (see our lined drape project in Chapter 15). Some of the window fabrics least prone to sun rot are chintzes, brocades, and cotton canvas.

✔ **Thread count:** One factor that makes a fabric stronger and last longer is its *thread count*, which is basically the number of *yarns* (the threads) in the *warp* (the lengthwise threads) and *weft* (the widthwise threads). Generally speaking, decorator fabrics have a higher thread count than fabrics used for making clothes, so decorator fabrics last a bit longer. Some of these fabrics need to be dry-cleaned; check the fabric bolt tag or cylinder tag.

✔ **Weave:** The weave of a fabric contributes to its look: Plain, twill, satin, or damask weaves are common ones for decorator fabrics. Most printed cottons are plain or twill weave. For example, satin weaves are used to create stripes in some fabrics, and a damask weave is a single-color, patterned weave.

The way a fabric is woven also contributes to its durability; generally, the more tightly woven a fabric, the more durable. More tightly woven fabrics also keep light out better, so keep that in mind when shopping.

✔ **Width:** Fabric generally comes in two basic widths: 42 to 45 inches and 54 to 60 inches. Always check out the fabric bolt label or tag to determine its width. Home-decorating fabrics compared to fabrics used for clothing are in the wider width. You can also find some decorating fabrics that are 72 to 75 inches wide, 90 inches wide, and even some that measure 105 or 110 inches or wider.

If you're dressing a small window, fabric width isn't that much of an issue. However, when you need to treat a large window or a bank of a few windows, lack of fabric width can become a problem. We recommend that you limit your search to the widest fabrics available. Our advice doesn't mean that you can't sew beautiful draperies with 45-inch-wide fabric. Just remember that if you choose to use that width that you'll spend more money and take more time. In order to get adequate width, you have to sew two or more widths of fabric together. If you're using a sheer fabric, you need more fullness and more width to achieve that look, too. Check out our Yardage Conversion Table in the Cheat Sheet in the front of this book to understand how moving across the range of fabric widths works.

When joining two or even three pieces of fabric together to get adequate coverage for a window treatment, remember that if you choose a printed fabric with a medium- or large-motif pattern, you need to match the pattern repeats from panel to panel. Unless you feel comfortable in your sewing skills, stick with a solid fabric, or choose a small, nondirectional (all-over) pattern. We discuss matching prints a bit later in this chapter in the "Picking prints carefully" section. See Chapters 6 and 10 for more on this topic.

Meeting your design needs

Still not sure what kind of fabric to choose? Here are a few familiar window treatment situations and recommendations for picking the right fabric.

A bank of wide, long windows that need plenty of coverage

Fabrics with some heft to them will meet your coverage needs. Make simple floor-to-ceiling panel draperies in a heavier-weight fabric, such as velvet, velveteen, corduroy, or a wool-blend fabric that limit the light. An alternative is to line your draperies with cotton duck.

For a less formal room, try crisscross curtains (see Chapter 14). When their tiebacks are removed, you'll get double coverage when one curtain falls over the other. For a more formal room, try pleated draperies (see Chapter 15) in a mediumweight cotton or blend.

A bank of wide, long windows where not much coverage is needed

A swag and cascade (see Chapter 15) made out of a nonsheer fabric with great drapability, such as a silk or blended charmeuse or a silk alternative (see the "Mediumweight fabric" section earlier in this chapter), that frames the top and sides of a bank of windows is a perfect treatment to provide some dress-up without much coverage. If you want to use a sheer fabric to diffuse the light, choose panels in gauze, batiste, organza, chiffon, or even lace.

A small room with drafty windows

Your design task is two-fold, but not that hard to solve. Think about adding a drapery that covers the window in its entirety. Measure your drapery so that it extends well past the window's trim molding. Then choose a heavier fabric, such as damask, in a color that matches (or closely matches) the room's paint color. The window treatment helps block cold air. Matching the fabric with the room's walls gives the room-enlarging illusion of unbroken wall space.

A very low-ceilinged room

Measure your draperies so they extend from the floor to the ceiling and match their color to the wall color. Be sure to install the curtain rod nearly flush with the ceiling. This classic decorator's trick creates the illusion of height in a room. If you want to let in light, choose a fabric whose texture is very light yet crisp, such as voile. If you like coverage, choose a tightly woven cotton. Using a fabric that features vertical stripes is another nice way you can create a feeling of length and height in a low-ceilinged room. Because the stripes are vertical, you can easily match the fabric panel to panel.

A small window, the only source of light in a small kitchen

If you have a small kitchen with only a tiny window, you want to maximize the window as much as possible. Consider adding a simple valance, or if you have the ceiling height, an arched valance (see Chapter 14) in the mediumweight fabric of your choice. Doing so enables you to take advantage of the light while still adding a bit of flourish without overwhelming the smaller window. For privacy in the evenings, you can add a simple roll-down shade, mounted out of sight under the valance for daytime. Another alternative is our double cafe curtain project in Chapter 14, which doesn't overwhelm a small window. Consider choosing a mediumweight fabric, such as gingham, challis, or toile, for cafe curtains. They have adequate weight to hang properly.

Blah-looking windows in a formal dining room that doubles as a study

Balloon valances (see Chapter 14) look great over sheers in dining rooms, and this treatment lets in adequate light for dining, working, or studying while adding a bit of design pizzazz. Choose a fabric with a tight weave and even a bit of stiffness when creating balloon valances (like chintz or taffeta), so they'll keep their shape. Nobody loves a limp balloon!

A bathroom window that needs privacy but still needs natural light

Some sheer fabrics are too sheer to do the trick. Try a heavier voile or plissé, which both give a bit of coverage, yet let in some light too. Plissé fabric comes in solids or patterns. Create a simple curtain panel (like the casement curtains in Chapter 14) with this fabric, and your problems are solved. When considering plissé, test a sample before pretreating; some plissés lose their texture when washed.

Slipping into a Comfortable, Sturdy Slipcover

Choosing a fabric for your new slipcover doesn't have to be a chore. A beautiful fabric — in a medium- or even a heavyweight, with a texture, pattern, and color you like, and the durability factors you need — is out there waiting for you. This section can help you decide which one is right for you.

Making an informed slipcover fabric choice

Think about these factors when you begin to decide on your slipcover fabric. If your head starts to spin when faced with myriad choices, having the basic necessities clearly in mind can keep you on the right track.

- **Added treatments:** Check to see whether the fabric has been treated with a stain- or flame-resistant or other type of finish. Some people like these additives and the utilitarian qualities they bring; others hate the smell that these additives can impart. Added treatments aren't an issue for window treatments as much as they are for slipcovers, because you don't lounge on your windows. If you have a chemically sensitive family member, read the bolt or cylinder tags carefully.

✔ **Colorfastness:** Choosing colorfastness is something to keep in mind. If your slipcover will be exposed to the sun all day, you want to pick a light or neutral color, which fades less quickly than a dark or bright color.

✔ **Texture:** Texture is an important issue to think about, because you'll be sitting and/or lounging on your slipcover. Linen is a traditional choice for slipcovers, but it may be too scratchy for your taste. Shiny fabrics such as satin and chintz reflect light and add a feeling of brightness, but they can be cold to the touch. Dull, matte, or napped fabrics such as wool or wool blends, velvet, and chenille are cozier and softer, but absorb light, so consider going for a brighter version of the color you have your heart set on. Crisp and stiff fabrics don't mold well to curves in your furniture, so avoid them unless the piece you're treating is all angles and lines. Very soft or sheer fabrics may be too slippery. Take home a sample — or even a full yard — of your fabric and get to know it before you decide.

✔ **Washability:** If you're blessed with the pitter-patter of little feet — human, canine, feline, or otherwise — you need a miracle fabric that hides dirt, food, and fur, or one that's easy to throw in the washing machine — sometimes even once a week. Plain or patterned denim, canvas, or even some types of tightly woven Jacquards may be just what you're looking for. Check the bolt tag on any fabric you're considering to determine its washability.

✔ **Weave:** A fabric with a tight weave stands up to everyday usage better than a loosely woven fabric. It keeps its shape and repels dirt and stains. Test for a tight weave by holding it up to the light. If you have a sample at home, pull at either side to determine how much *give* (notable movement of fibers) it has.

✔ **Weight:** One of the most important things to look for in slipcover fabric is the correct weight. Deciding on a light-, medium-, or heavyweight fabric (refer to "Weighing Your Fabric Options" earlier in this chapter for details) is partly a choice based on the function of the slipcover and partly a choice based on how comfortable you are handling and using a sewing machine with different weight fabric.

Cotton or cotton-blend fabrics, such as chintz and toile or a silk or cotton damask, are easier to work with in mediumweights than in heavyweights; choose them for a less-used, formal area. A slipcover for a well-used piece of furniture — your family room or den sofa — might last longer in a heavier fabric, such as denim, corduroy, velvet or velveteen, or even brocade. If you don't feel confident in how you or your sewing machine will handle a heavyweight fabric, try a mediumweight version of a tight-weave fabric, such as denim.

✔ **Width:** Fabric width is important to keep in mind when you're making your choice. Decorator fabrics come in a standard 54- to 60-inch width, but you may be able to find fabrics even wider, in some cases 105 to 110 inches wide. Narrower widths are usually reserved for clothing, so we can't recommend them for large projects because of the cost.

Other important factors to consider

Some fabrics, although simply gorgeous, for one reason or another just aren't cut out for making slipcovers. Some fabrics split, tear, or stretch when you actually use your furniture. Others are quite expensive and thus may be prohibitively expensive for covering an entire loveseat or sofa when you're on a budget. However, some great fabrics are available for making slipcovers, and you need to be able to find one that suits your needs.

In general, we recommend the following fabrics wholeheartedly for slipcovers:

- ✔ Cotton or blended denim or duck
- ✔ Cotton, polyester, or blended brocades and brocatelles
- ✔ Cotton or polyester chenille
- ✔ Cotton or polyester velvet
- ✔ Cotton velveteen or corduroy
- ✔ Printed cottons, such as toile or chintz
- ✔ Silk, cotton, or blended damask
- ✔ Tapestry fabrics
- ✔ Ultrasuede or other faux-suede microfiber
- ✔ Wool or wool blend

However, you need to size up your own needs and wants and factor them into your final decision.

Spicing up your sofa with seasonal slipcovers

You can give your sofa a new look every time the seasons change. Making three or even four different seasonal slipcovers for one sofa isn't only stylish, it's economical. What at first seems like an inordinate amount of work (and an expensive financial proposition) may actually turn out to be a cheap and easy solution to the dreaded problem of looking at the same old sofa year in and year out or a stylish way to protect a valuable antique. Making a few slipcovers is, of course, cheaper than buying new sofas and much less hassle than moving them in and out of a room (not to mention storing them). And because you'll be rotating slipcovers every three or four months or so, the slipcovers will last a long time.

For spring, you may want to choose a lightweight fabric with a pattern that reflects the renewal of nature. For summer, a crisp, light solid may work. For fall/winter, a deeper-toned, heftier fabric works, because most people tend to spend more time inside (and in the couch-potato position) during colder months.

When creating reversible slipcovers (see Chapter 17), always select two fabrics of equal weight. If the weights of your two fabrics are different, your slipcover may not hang properly nor launder well. Your best bet is choosing two colors or patterns from the same fabric family, for example two denims, one printed and one solid.

Coordinating your colors

Your furniture slipcovers need to complement your room, of course, but they also serve as a style element with which you can elaborate on a theme. You can echo colors from elsewhere in the room or break out with something bold and different yet still harmonious. Pick a color palette that matches your room and generally stay within its parameters, or pick out another color entirely based on the cool/warm paradigm we talk about in Chapter 1.

Color intensifies when you use a lot of it. For example, the fabric you're considering for covering a small stool or ottoman won't elicit the same effect as the fabric you choose for a full-size sofa or a prominent armchair. Remember this concept especially when choosing "in-between" colors, like chartreuse (part yellow/part green), magenta (part pink/part purple), or fluorescent colors. A little of these colors goes a long way, so you may want to use them as trims or accents instead of as the main color choice.

Some people shy away from light-toned fabric for slipcovers because they think they show dirt, and they avoid white like the plague for the same reason. In our way of thinking, the dirt is still there even if you can't see it, so you may as well deal with it so why not go with a light-toned fabric if it fits your palette. If you choose a good-quality, washable cotton fabric, for example, you can use color-safe bleach or bleach alternative to remove stains without fear.

Keep a *color notebook* — which is just a blank notebook with samples of the paint colors you've used in your rooms and swatches of fabrics you've used to decorate. If you can't get fabric swatches, consider attaching a Polaroid or clear close-up photographs of your furniture, or better yet, the whole room. Your color notebook can help you match your new fabric to the colors you already have in the room and your house. (You don't have to spend a lot of money on your color notebook. You can simply use a spiral notebook, some tape or glue, a pen to label the samples and swatches, and presto!)

Picking prints carefully

If you're creating only one slipcover for your sofa, we recommend that you use a solid fabric (or a subtle, petite-scaled print). You won't get tired of a solid as quickly as you will a print, and you can always change accent pillows on a solid slipcover for a brand-new look.

Working with medium- or large-scale prints, stripes, or plaids can be a sewing challenge. Matching them from panel to panel, and especially on furniture where you must sew a curvy seam is difficult and you'll probably have to buy more fabric to do it right. However, if you prefer using a print, keep in mind that prints can be one-way or nondirectional:

- *One-way* means the pattern only looks right when viewed one way. For example, a blooming rose with a stem underneath it only looks right when viewed with the blossoms heading north and the stem heading south. You have to lay your fabric out so that each piece is cut this way. When joining two pieces of fabric together to make a wide panel, you need to make sure the spacing between the roses is always consistent.

- *Nondirectional* means you don't have to look at the print from any certain direction (for instance, polka dots). Choosing a nondirectional design is better. When you pin and tuck fabric, you get a cohesive look. When you cut and sew with a pattern, you don't have to worry about matching motifs.

If you want to try a medium-size print with the tucked-and-pinned projects in Chapter 11, we recommend something like an alternating 1-inch stripe with two colors, because it results in a funky, multidirectional effect that's fun.

For projects where you have to match pattern parts, like those in Chapters 16 and 17, matching medium- or large-scale prints on a loveseat or sofa can be very difficult. You need to be skilled at matching patterns at their seams and plan ahead of time where they fall within each section of your sofa. Each time you position your pattern, make sure the fabric underneath is identical to the previous pattern. We discuss this concept a bit more in Chapters 6 and 10. For more information on working with one-way patterns, see *Sewing For Dummies,* 2nd edition, by Jan Saunders Maresh (Wiley).

Uneven stripes and uneven plaids are tough to match for slipcovers. Unless you have a bit of experience with "unevens," look for fabric where all the stripes are the same width (use your tape measure if you're not sure).

To find out whether a plaid design is even, fold the fabric in half the long way and then turn back a corner, so that it's folded on the bias. If the top and bottom layer form mirror images of each other, you have an even plaid, and if they don't, you have an uneven plaid. The same goes for stripes.

If you choose a print with a small pattern, say, a half-inch or so, you'll have better luck matching each pattern piece or section of your slipcover. However, if the repeat is larger, say 2 inches or even 4 inches, you have to make sure the repeats match, and to be able to do so, you may need to buy much more fabric. Keep these factors in mind when you're choosing and shopping for fabric. (See Chapter 10 for more on measuring fabric with prints.)

Chapter 3

Buying, Pretreating, and Caring for Your Fabrics

In This Chapter

▶ Arming yourself with info to make a knowledgeable purchase

▶ Checking out places to buy fabric

▶ Determining how much fabric to buy and whether you can afford it

▶ Using bed sheets for your treatments and slipcovers

▶ Pretreating your fabric after you bring it home

▶ Making your finished window treatments and slipcovers last with proper care

*I*f you haven't spent a bit of time thinking about the fabric type that's perfect for your project, then check out Chapter 2. If you have, the next step is to go out, find it, and acquire the correct amount at the right price. Equally important is caring for your fabric before you begin to sew, as well as after your project is complete.

In this chapter, we discuss the ins and outs of selecting fabric at a variety of stores, and offer you some alternative fabric sources, as well. We give some advice on figuring out your fabric needs and tips on sticking to a budget. We also recommend some unconventional fabric sources and tell you what you need to know about pretreating, washing, and drying your fabric.

Gathering Info — At Home and at the Store

Spending time browsing in fabric stores to familiarize yourself with fabrics can be fun and edifying. It can also help you formulate your decorating plan. But when you're ready to buy, it pays to arm yourself with the necessary information.

That's why we say that the simple maxim "Know before you go" is essential when making fabric choices. If you can plan at home and decide beforehand what style, color, and texture fabric to buy, you can make your job much easier and much more fun, not to mention time saving (you don't have to go back again and again) and space saving (no stacking fabric in a closet for "future" projects that you may never make).

Figuring out what you need

Having the answers to these questions in this section in mind (or jotted down in your color notebook; see Chapter 2) before you go shopping for fabric for window treatments and/or slipcovers can save you time, money, and frustration.

For window treatments

This list of questions can help you narrow your search for the perfect fabric to treat your windows.

- ✔ How much light do you want to allow in, or how much do you want to keep out?

- ✔ Do the windows you plan to treat face north, south, east, or west?

    If the window is in a bedroom and faces east, you may want a heavier fabric to keep the sunlight out for those mornings when you want to sleep in.

- ✔ Does this room accommodate temperamental sleepers?

- ✔ Do you want to filter, but not block out light?

- ✔ How much privacy do you need, and will the room you're treating benefit from a bit of noise control?

    A heavier, fuller treatment ensures privacy, as well as muffles outside elements.

- ✔ How much weight can your window and decor support?

    A small room with a small window benefits from a treatment that is, you guessed it . . . small! A room of grander proportion and large or long windows does well with a more dramatic treatment.

For slipcovers

The following questions can help you as you decide on appropriate fabric to cover your furniture.

✔ How do you plan on using the slipcover?

- Will you nap on it each Sunday? If so, make sure you love the feel of the fabric you choose.

- Will your pet climb on it or child play on it? If so, make sure the fabric is durable and doesn't snag on toys or pet's nails.

- Will you just be placing clothes or lingerie on it? If so, consider a lightweight fabric, as long as it offers enough coverage so the original design doesn't peak through.

✔ How often does this slipcover need spot-cleaning, and how often a real wash?

Some slipcovers require more cleaning because they're used more often. For example, slipcovers for dining room tables get food on them, and people snack on den sofas in front of the TV, but ottomans will probably receive fewer stains.

✔ How committed are you to working with a printed fabric?

Matching medium or large prints can be a challenge for a novice.

For both

The following are important considerations to contemplate whether you're creating a new window treatment or a slipcover, or both. If you plan to match your window fabric to your slipcover fabric, read on.

✔ Which tones or colors in your room decor do you want to echo with the window treatment or slipcover?

If you make this decision early on, especially whether you're going for a solid or a print, you can narrow your search considerably. (See Chapter 1 for an in-depth discussion of color.)

✔ Are you sure of the correct amount of fabric for your project, and can you get more if you need to?

If you do need more, can the store order more for you, or is there another store location where you can get additional yardage? Keep in mind that dye lots vary. (The vats in which fabrics are dyed are supposed to be consistent, but even the slightest change in dye amount due to minor human error can make two pieces of fabric with the same style and color number look quite different.) Make sure if you have to return for more fabric, that you can match your fabric perfectly. If you can't, be sure to buy enough the first time.

✔ How much fabric can you afford?

(See "Deciding How Much Fabric You Need (and Can Afford)" later in this chapter for some great tips.)

Chatting with your friendly salesperson

Your best fabric-choosing resources (besides this wonderful book) are the salespeople at fabric stores, fabric outlets, and wholesale establishments (we talk about these different places in the "Shopping for Fabrics in the Right Location" section later in this chapter). The men and women who own and work at these stores are around fabric all day long, and many of them are very knowledgeable sewers. Some of them are second- or third-generation fabric folks. Questions you can — and should — ask include

✔ What's the widest decorating fabric you stock?

✔ Can you recommend a sheer window fabric, preferably one that won't pill or wrinkle if I need to wash it often?

✔ How many different weight brocades can you show me? Which is the thinnest, and which is the thickest?

✔ Can you recommend a microfiber fabric appropriate for a heavily used slipcover?

Don't be afraid to find out something new from professionals. Let them do their job and show off their knowledge a bit. You may discover something new.

Rolling out the bolts

At the fabric store, don't be shy about rolling out the fabric *bolt* (the cardboard flats or round tubes upon which the fabric is stored) and taking a long look at what you may be buying. Nobody will give you a funny look if you do. As a matter of fact, most people won't give you a second glance because they'll think you really know how to shop for fabric. The reason for rolling out the bolts is three-fold. You want

✔ **To make sure that the fabric has been dyed evenly and consistently, and that the overall effect of the color is the one you want.** You can't determine these consistencies with just a foot or so of fabric showing, so open the bolt wide.

✔ **To check the fabric on the bolt for small holes and fabric inconsistencies.** Fabrics with unusual weaves can disguise such flaws, and some fabrics, such as doupioni and shantung silk, have *slubs* (tiny irregularities in the fiber that give the fabric texture and personality) and other "flaws." Tightly woven and shiny-finished fabrics (cottons or cotton blends or sateens) show their flaws immediately. You can probably see them with 2 or 3 yards showing.

✔ **To see how the fabric behaves.** For example, does it drape well (if you're creating a swag)? Is it stiff enough to hold pleats in place (for a pleated treatment)?

If you choose to accept a bolt of fabric that features more than a few flaws (perhaps to save money, or because it's a one-of-a-kind fabric), be sure to add an additional 5 percent of your total fabric needs to make up for fabric lost to these flaws. Or you can plan to cover the flaws with appliqués or other decorative accessories; see Chapters 8 and 12 for more information.

You can see that we're slightly prejudiced toward only buying your fabric sight seen (see the sidebar "The risks of buying online" later in this chapter about buying fabric online). By buying your fabric in person, you can thoroughly inspect it for any flaws and save time and money in the long run.

Taking some fabric home

When you're doubting whether a fabric is the right one, ask for a *swatch* (a small sample piece) of fabric to take home. Pin or tape the sample to your window or furniture, and then stand back to admire it. For window treatments, make sure you view your potential fabric at the same distance at which you'll be living with it (for example, from the sofa or dining room table). For both window treatments and slipcovers, note how the color or colors work with your decor, how the scale of the print works with any other prints in the room, and how the light changes the fabric's appearance throughout the day.

For an even better idea of how a particular fabric will block light, buy a half-yard, pin it up on your rod or tape it to the top of your window frame, and stand back. Again, see how the sun shines through it at different times of the day and consider its color(s) and/or print carefully.

When picking up fabric samples, always copy the name and number of the fabric, the fiber content, the laundering instructions (if provided), and any repeat size information (if applicable; this is the distance in inches between like motifs on print fabrics) from the fabric bolt or tag, and the store name into your color notebook (see Chapter 2), so you know where to find it in case you later decide to buy it.

If you're worried about the care and tending of your future creation, you can now test it to see how it responds in different situations. For example,

- ✔ Pretreat it according to the cleaning directions on the label's bolt. (See "Pretreating: A Must for Happy Fabrics" later in this chapter for more information on pretreating fabrics). Don't be afraid to test the fabric sample a bit roughly.

- ✔ Splash a bit of water on your fabric samples that specifically call for dry-cleaning only, and see how incoming raindrops might stain them.

- ✔ Add a bit of dirt to your fabric and see how it comes out with spot-cleaning. Better to know now than later if you don't want to invest in high-maintenance draperies or a slipcover that you can't wash, even in cold water.

✔ Check to see how your potential fabric reacts to spilled milk, dog hair, or any other day-to-day utilitarian challenges it may face. If you plan on making a drapery-length treatment, especially one that puddles on the ground, let your child or pet get a hold of it as well, because they're sure to find the fabric after it's up on your windows.

If your favorite window treatment fabric isn't as functional as you were hoping, consider lining it with cotton duck, which blocks light and provides insulation for not a lot of money (see Chapter 16 to discover how to make lined draperies).

Shopping for Fabrics in the Right Location

For people who love fabric, seeking it out is one of best parts of starting a new sewing project. People who horde fabric, always declaring some "future project" as an excuse for keeping tons of extra fabric around, know how much fun taking out their fabrics and looking at them every once in a while can be, then imagining them on a pillow, up on a window, or covering a chair.

You've never had as many fabric shopping choices as you do today. In this section we talk about where to shop for fabric — at fabric stores, outlets, and online — and what to expect.

The fabric store

The different types of fabric stores range from the high-end store that sells nondiscounted, expensive, (and sometimes imported) fabric to the low-end discount store that sells fabric at low prices. Each type has its advantages. One of the benefits of shopping at high-end fabric stores is that the fabric is beautifully displayed. You can easily find everything, and fabrics are usually grouped together by types, so you can contrast and compare a variety of manufacturers. Low-end stores try to group their goods, but it's usually a bit more of a hodge podge. You have to do a bit more exploring to find what you want, but if you find what you're looking for, you pay a lot less.

Fabric stores offer literally hundreds of fabrics to choose from the leading fabric manufacturers. They also offer a mind-boggling array of trims, as well as all the standard sewing accoutrements, such as pattern paper, needles, scissors, and measuring tapes. Being able to buy your fabric and trim at the same place saves you valuable time and money. You can compare colors and textures at the same time without having to run all over town.

Lifestyles of the rich

You can go to fabric showrooms, accompanied by a designer or interior decorator only, and peruse fabrics at your leisure while chatting with the knowledgeable staff. A fabric showroom is the clothing boutique version of fabric buying. Even with the to-the-trade courtesy your decorator gets, a fabric showroom is still much more expensive than going on your own to a store (and nice if you can afford it). The advantages are access to exclusive fabric lines and expert advice that make your fabric shopping experience a breeze.

Fabric stores also offer their customers memo and swatch services. *Memos* are larger pieces of fabric that you can borrow (for a nominal fee) and return later. You can't pretreat or misuse these fabric samples, so no stretching or throwing water on them! *Swatches* are small fabric samples that you can take home for free. (We recommend, however, that if you think a fabric may be "the one" after borrowing a memo or taking home a small swatch, that you purchase a half yard and live with it for a few days. Pretreat it and handle it as it shall be in its slipcover or window treatment incarnation.

Fabric stores also offer other advantages. Talk with the staff and check out a fabric store's Web site for tips and information on sewing classes and special guest speakers who can teach you some tricks of the trade.

We really recommend that you buy your fabric off the same bolt, because dye lots can vary. Fabric stores can be very helpful in the terrible event that you run out of fabric. Before you panic, go to the store to see if it has more in stock (keep your receipt so you can refer to the fabric number and color). If the store doesn't, a salesperson may be able to call another store or get in touch with the manufacturer directly.

Fabric outlets

Fabric outlets stock a variety of discounted fabrics — usually at least 30 percent to 60 percent off or more. You can easily identify these stores because they usually have the word "discount," "outlet," or "bargain" in their name. Some are small and have more of a traditional store feeling, while others have a big warehouse vibe.

Fabric outlets generally have a decent selection at a discount. When shopping at an outlet, buy what you need when you see it. Often, if these places run out of one fabric, it may never come back again. Plan accordingly. These stores also have a decent selection of trims and other accessories, but they're usually going out of production, so get all you need before you leave the store. Outlets don't discount notions and sewing needs that don't go out of style, such as scissors, pins, and more.

Scrounging for remnants

Remnants are end-of-bolt pieces that may only be a yard or two of fabric. Fabric stores and outlets put them in piles because they take up too much room on the shelves, and they sell them at a low price. They're the equivalent of Sunday dinner's leftovers — still tasty, but insufficient for a large meal.

The advantage of buying remnants is they're so cheap! If you're making an accent pillow for your sofa, a remnant may be perfect. They're also great for mixing and matching prints, and for making contrasting tiebacks for curtains or drapes. If you're good with the sewing machine, you can often get your total yardage by adding up a few smaller pieces. Getting enough to cover a whole sofa or a large window, however, may be a challenge.

Furthermore, you usually don't find anything "wrong" with the fabrics the outlet is selling. To be on the safe side though, check outlet fabrics for minor damage, such as fading or flaws. In fact, many outlets offer the lower prices simply because

✔ They're overstocked, meaning the store ordered too much (swayed by some overzealous salesperson, no doubt).

✔ The fabrics are from last year's collection.

✔ The fabrics didn't appeal to the general public's taste, and are being discontinued to make way for new fabric.

Because stores have to rotate and add new merchandise to keep customers interested, fabric has a shelf life, just as fashion does.

Look at your trip to a fabric outlet store as an adventure. You're on the hunt for the perfect fabric. Wear comfortable shoes because many outlets tend to be less organized than regular fabric stores. You may spend some time walking long aisles and digging through bolts and remnant tables in pursuit of the flawless bargain. After you find that perfect fabric though, the entire scavenger hunt will all be worth it.

Also keep in mind that some domestic linen outlets carry brand-name and designer tablecloths and sheets that are often marked "irregular." *Irregular items* have some slight imperfections that most people don't even notice. If something is marked irregular, double-check the seams. You could spend a frustrating hour trying to get a straight cut only to discover that the manufacturer couldn't get it right either.

Online fabric companies

The Internet is another great source for fabric (we recommend a few online fabric companies in Chapter 20). By doing a search for a specific fabric type, you may hit on a company that specializes in silks, denims, brocades, or vinyl, thus simplifying your search. What could be easier than narrowing down fabrics by style, color, or width with a click of your mouse?

When buying from an online company, be sure it has an excellent business rating and offers a money-back guarantee. To protect their reputation, quality online dealers treat their fabric and customers with equal regard. Reputable online fabric companies always cut your fabric from the same bolt.

Many online fabric stores have a swatch service that we recommend you take advantage of. They take a few days to arrive, so it does add some waiting to your project-making timeframe. Ask for swatches of fabrics you're considering, so you can confirm that the color or colors you're seeing on your computer screen are true (usually they're not). Seeing, feeling, and comparing the fabrics before you make a big purchase are important steps.

Shopping for basics, such as cotton batting, scissors, and needles, over the Internet can be very cost effective. Because many of these companies don't have to pay the overhead for a storefront, you can get warehouse-style savings.

The risks of buying online

Although you can find some good bargains while shopping for fabric online, buying fabric online has all the disadvantages of a computer dating service. Though you can see the fabric, or a computer-created version of it, you can't touch the fabric, and that may be a deal breaker for some people. And when the real thing shows up at your door, it may not be all it's cracked up to be.

If you have a bit of sewing experience and are familiar with a type of fabric and have used it successfully before, then by all means, shop online. If you're a fabric novice and don't know quite what to expect from a certain fabric, look for the contact information on the site and e-mail or call the company's customer service representative and have a chat about what you're thinking of purchasing. Inquire about the return policies while you have someone on the line.

Some fabric Web sites are just extensions of "real" fabric stores, another opportunity for businesspeople to expand their trade. Look for companies that have been in business for a number of years. That bit of information ideally means satisfied customers, which means good-quality fabric. Only deal with an online vendor that offers a fabric swatch service, where you can confirm color, because computer monitors aren't accurate.

Other places to find fabric

You may also find that perfect fabric you need for your window treatments and slipcover at nontraditional locations instead of a typical fabric store. The following are just a few examples of places to look:

- ✔ **Flea markets, church bazaars, garage sales, and thrift shops:** Visiting these types of places may be worth your time and money. Some have fabric for sale, but you can also look at large-size coats, dresses, and other clothing with an eye toward cutting up and reusing the fabric. You may find just enough of one fabric (lace on an otherwise hideous blouse, for example) you love to create wonderful tiebacks — for a couple of bucks!

  If you're fortunate enough to find some beautiful fabric at a flea market, thrift store, garage sale, or bazaar, an added challenge is finding enough fabric to treat an entire window or slipcover a chair. However you may get lucky and find that perfect fabric, and get a fun story to tell when guests compliment your work, too.

- ✔ **Indian women's clothing stores:** If you're lucky enough to live near an Indian or other Southeast Asian community, you may want to visit one or a few of the women's clothing stores in the area, where you can find an array of colorful sari fabrics. These, long, scarf-like garments are perfect for creating swag treatments as well as some simple flat or shirred panel treatments, such as casement curtains.

  While you're in the neighborhood, check out any fabric stores, where you're sure to find some beautiful imported fabric. India is world renowned for its textile work and with good reason. The handiwork — beads of all types, tiny mirrors, sequins, and embroidery — is second to none.

Deciding How Much Fabric You Need (and Can Afford)

Finding a fabric in the correct quantity and for the right price can sometimes be a challenge. Sure, if you waltz into a high-end decorating shop, you can find scads of beautiful fabrics in abundance, but you'll also pay through the nose. The other side of the coin is shopping at an outlet, where the fabric is the right price, but you may not find one that's truly special.

The first step to getting the best of both worlds is to understand what you're looking at when you pick up a bolt of fabric. You need to understand what widths fabrics come in and the normal pricing per yard of both high- and low-end fabrics. Don't worry. This section can give you several tips and pointers so your next trip to the fabric store is a successful one.

Sizing up your fabric needs

Fabric is woven in several conventional widths: 36 inches; 42 to 45 inches; 54, 58, and 60 inches; 75, 90, and in some cases, 105 to 110 inches. The narrow widths are usually reserved for clothing; however, some wonderful ethnic fabrics are 36 or 45 inches wide.

The fabric bolt, or hangtag on a cylinder bolt, is where the manufacturer lists all the information you need to know about the fabric, including fiber content, fabric width, and whether the fabric has been prewashed. Pattern-repeat length is indicated on the bolt or cylinder tag as well.

If you're making a sofa slipcover, you definitely want to go with the 54-to-60-inch width, or if you can find it, 105 or 110-inch-wide fabrics that can save you a lot of sewing. (Who wants to sew a bunch of small panels of fabric together?) Always check the info on the fabric bolt or on a cylinder bolt's hangtag to determine the fabric's dimensions, or ask the salesperson to double-check the width before cutting the cloth. Always remember: As soon as the salesperson cuts the fabric, consider it sold.

If the fabric you like is made from natural fibers or a blend with natural fibers, and hasn't been prewashed, you must allow for some initial shrinkage when calculating how much fabric you need. To be on the safe side, if you're making a project that needs a lot of fabric — a sofa slipcover or even a very long or wide pair of drapes — adding an extra 3 yards to accommodate shrinkage is a good idea. For more on this topic, see "Pretreating: A Must for Happy Fabrics" later in this chapter.

For window treatments

Each project has specific measuring information, but in this section we give you a quick overview on measuring to help you figure out how much solid-colored or small-print, nondirectional print fabric you need for a basic window panel.

The total amount of fabric you need for a window treatment depends on your treatment's finished dimension, not your window frame, because most treatments extend past the frame.

To begin calculating yardage for your window:

1. **Measure your window treatment width.**

   You decide where your treatment will extend — to the edge of the frame, 1 inch outside the frame, or even 3 or more inches, depending on the look you're after. Measure from the edge of the extension on one side to the edge of the extension on the other side of the window. Divide the total in half if your treatment will separate in the middle.

For most treatments that require fullness, the fabric for your width needs to be 2½ times the width of this measurement.

Add 2 inches if you plan to have ½-inch side hems, 4 inches if you plan to have 1-inch side hems.

2. **For your length, measure from the top of your mounted rod or pole to where you want your treatment to end (usually at the sill, halfway below the sill, to the floor, or farther, if you seek a *puddle* effect, where the fabric cascades onto the floor to create the look of, you guessed it, a puddle).**

For your top and bottom hem, double the measurement of your desired hem depth and add it to the total length. For example, for a 1-inch hem, add 2 inches.

3. **To calculate the *heading* (the extra, decorative fabric that extends above the rod sleeve or other casing), if necessary, double the desired measurement.**

For example, for a 3-inch heading, add 6 inches to your length.

Be sure to calculate for any rings or other hardware you plan to use when figuring total length.

For more information, refer to specific projects in this book, where we talk about fabric quantities, and check out the measuring information in Chapter 6.

For slipcovers

This section includes an approximate breakdown of how much solid or small, nondirectional print (that is, no-repeat print) fabric you need for slipcover projects:

- ✔ **A large sofa:** 10 to 14 yards of 60-inch-wide fabric or 16 to 20 yards of 45-inch-wide fabric

- ✔ **A small sofa:** 6 to 8 yards of 60-inch-wide fabric or 10 to 12 yards of 45-inch-wide fabric

- ✔ **A small table:** 5 to 6 yards of 60-inch-wide fabric or 6 to 8 yards of 45-inch-wide fabric

- ✔ **A standard-size armchair:** 4 to 6 yards of 60-inch-wide fabric or 8 to 10 yards of 45-inch-wide fabric

- ✔ **A dining room chair:** 3 yards of either 45-inch-wide or 60-inch-wide fabric.

- ✔ **An ottoman:** 2 yards of either 45- or 60-inch-wide fabric

If you've initially planned to use a 60-inch-wide fabric, but can find only a 45-inch-wide fabric that really pleases you, just add between 4 and 6 extra yards of fabric. For a smaller sofa, use 4 yards, and for a larger sofa, use 6 yards. If you're lucky enough to find a fabric you like that is 110 inches wide, you'll need a little more than half the estimated yardage for the 60-inch-wide fabric estimates in the previous bulleted list. Check out the Yardage Conversion Table in the Cheat Sheet at the beginning of this book for more on going from one width of fabric to another.

Pricing fabrics

Everyone loves a bargain, and yet sometimes you just can't get a good deal on fabric to save your life. Some stubborn fabrics are like that; they're just plain expensive. For example, you're just not going to find silk Jacquards and taffetas for $5 a yard, not even on a sale day. High-end fabrics, and hand-worked and beaded fabrics are astronomical in price, and the gamut runs down to low-end fabric, such as simple printed synthetics and cottons that go for $6 or $7 a yard. But the truth is you can find some really fantastic fabric great for making window treatments and slipcovers in the range of $15 to $20 per yard.

The inside scoop on fabric prices

A few different factors can add up to a higher cost for your fabrics. Keep the following points in mind the next time your mouth is gaping at the price of that precious silk.

✔ **Fiber content is one way that price is determined.** The raw material to make the fabric — and the source for that raw material — can result in a high cost. Keeping an insect fed and comfortable while you wait around for it to spin its silky web can take some time and money (though those little guys don't eat *that* much). Even natural disasters can cause a shortage of natural fibers contributing to the price. A drought or an influx of hungry insects can hurt natural fiber production, which can be passed on to the consumer. Because of these ever-changing factors, fabrics like real silk always go for premium rates. A man-made imitation silk, on the other hand, made mostly of polyester, has the approximation of silk without the cost.

✔ **The laws of supply and demand in a free market can make fabric expensive.** A high demand for fabric raises its cost. Wedding dress silks are more expensive than other silks because each year, the world keeps churning out more brides (and bridesmaids!). In the same vein, if a new fabric has an exclusive licensing agreement, it will be more costly than one widely available and made by many manufacturers.

✔ **Some fabrics are expensive because they take more time to make.** Beautiful brocade spends a long time on the loom because the colors and designs are woven in, not simply printed on. Creating complicated or multi-colored designs on any type of fabric entails more man-hours, and guess who gets to pay for that labor!

✔ **The research behind the material matters.** When considering microfibers, you're paying for the investment in research by chemical companies, and then for the development of these new fabrics based on that research. Similarly, when you're buying a fabric created by a celebrity designer or a well-known design house, you're paying for their experience, name recognition, and label.

What you can expect pricewise

In general, most home-decorating fabrics bought at outlets cost from $7 to $25 per yard, with $15 being the average per-yard price for a nice, long-lasting fabric. Prices per yard may go up or down, depending on where you buy your fabric, so it pays to shop around. Also, keep in mind that obtaining the fabric width you need affects your project's total cost. Table 3-1 shows some per-yard price averages.

Table 3-1	Common Prices for Common Fabrics
Fabric/ Weight	*Price Per Yard*
Silk satins	$25 to $50
Silk taffetas	$25 to $50
Most silk velvets	$25 to $50
Most silk Jacquards, like damask and brocade	$15 to $30
Most cotton Jacquards, like damask and brocade	$10 to $30
Synthetic suede	$18 to $25
Medium- and heavyweight cotton velvets, corduroys, or velveteens	$15 to $25
Faux fur	$10 to $15
Most polyester velvets	$10 to $15
Silk chiffons	$10 to $15
Wool crepes	$10 to $15
Polyester lace	$8 to $15
Linen	$5 to $15
Mediumweight cotton prints, like chintz	$5 to $15
Polyester chenille	$5 to $15
Polyester satins	$5 to $15
Vinyl	$7 to $13
Polyester chiffons	$5 to $10
Cotton or cotton-blend denims	$5 to $10
Polyester crepes	$5 to $10
Most polyester taffetas	$5 to $10

Sewing on a budget

Sewing up a simple swag made from an inexpensive but pretty polyester blend fabric, or covering a little footstool or smaller ottoman with a remnant piece of tapestry fabric won't break the bank, but what if you're treating a large bank of windows or a matching sofa and loveseat? Most decorator fabrics are gorgeous, high-quality creations that are built to last, and many of them have high price tags to match. You may not be able to, or even want to, dedicate tons of money to every room in your home. If you're on a tight budget, keep these few points in mind before you commit to fabric:

✔ **Determine the total cost of creating your window treatment or slipcover at a few price points before you buy your fabric.** Consider the following costs for window treatments: fabric price per yard times total yards needed (including lining, if necessary), thread, trim, hardware, professional cleaning costs, if any, and any coordinating treatments that will complement what you're making (such as blinds, shutters, or shades that might go behind your treatment). Also be sure to factor in any tools (see Chapter 5) you need to buy to make the treatment, and finally, the cost of your time.

Consider the following for slipcovers: fabric, thread, trim, any accessories that you may need (see Chapter 13), professional cleaning costs, if any, additional tools, plus the cost of your time.

✔ **Always buy the best fabric you can afford, but if your budget is getting tight, consider a less-expensive alternative.** Place the two fabrics side by side and compare their qualities. Don't be afraid to ask a fabric store salesperson and be specific about your needs: "I like the color, print, and weight of this fabric. I don't need a fabric that has such a lustrous finish or soft feel. Do you have something very similar to this fabric, but in a lower price range?"

✔ **Consider fabric value.** For special slipcovers, you don't necessarily need a fabric that wears well on an everyday basis. If you're creating a holiday-only slipcover for your family room or den that will only be on your sofa one month out of the year, you can opt for a less durable fabric that still has a design that fits the bill. These special-print or novelty fabrics may be a little more money than a plain canvas or denim, but your slipcover will last a long time. What you lose in cost you gain in value.

✔ **How long will you keep your window treatment or slipcover in place?** If you redecorate frequently or plan to get new furniture in the future, or if the person who occupies the room you're treating has fickle tastes (can you say "teenager"?), perhaps a synthetic version of that opulent silk fabric may be in order. If you intend to stay put for a while or even retire in the home you're decorating, you can feel confident to go with a fabric that you really love.

✔ **Contemplate the room's use.** Are some rooms cordoned off to keep pets out? Are other rooms ones that young children are prohibited from entering? You may want to decorate with fabrics that are a bit more delicate in their care and a bit more expensive, instead of opting for a thrifty, durable fabric. Also, some rooms are more "public" than others, such as dining rooms and living rooms, so you may want to apply more of your decorating budget there, especially if you're required to entertain at home for business.

Don't let the higher cost of microfiber make you think you're getting a heavier fabric. Microfibers are actually much thinner than those of plant- or animal-derived fabrics, such as wool, linen, and even silk.

Stretching your dollar to the limit

You can see in Table 3-1 that picking a polyester version of a fabric classically made in a natural fiber can save you some money. However, synthetics aren't always going to be cheaper than natural fabrics. Some really fantastic, new-fangled synthetic fabrics are as costly as silks, and so are some very expensive polyester brocades. The best way to choose well-priced fabric doesn't mean choosing only synthetics or naturals, but rather shopping around and comparing prices. The following tips can help you snag a great deal.

✔ **Consider buying fabric with a wide selvage.** Sometimes a bolt of fabric is reduced in price because the *selvage* (the right or left finished edges) is too wide or uneven. If you plan to cover this edge with decorative trim, or trim it away entirely, an overlarge selvage isn't an issue. (See Chapters 9 and 13 for discussions about how to add trim and a bunch of other shortcuts and quick fixers.) For more ways to find an inexpensive fabric, check out the "Scrounging for remnants" sidebar in this chapter.

✔ **Try to cut a deal.** Sometimes if a fabric is at the end of its bolt, you can negotiate a deal for the last 2 or 3 yards, which can be really useful and economical when creating window treatments. For example, you can use a few yards for creating a contrasting ruffle or tieback, for adding some extra fabric at the bottom hem for a visual effect, for creating some needed weight, or for fixing length mistakes (you cut the fabric too short and need to lengthen the treatment).

The minimum amount of fabric that you can buy is a ½-yard, no less. Some stores maintain a 1-yard minimum, so ask first.

✔ **Combine fabrics.** Buy an inexpensive but durable fabric for your slip-cover, and a yard of ornate and expensive fabric for a coordinating pillow (or two, if you can squeak it out of one yard). The pillow makes the slip-cover look better, and you'll have the new, fresh look you've been craving.

Cheating with Sheets

If you hate to sew and hate to shop for fabric, but you're still committed to trying one or a few of the projects we offer in this book (specifically in Chapters 7 and 11), think about cheating — with flat sheets! They're great for our no-sew and low-sew projects because they offer several advantages:

✔ Their edges are already finished.

✔ They're usually wide enough to avoid joining several fabric panels together, which saves you mucho sewing time.

✔ They're multifunctional.

You can use the sheets in many different ways. For example, if you have leftover sheet fabric, you can use it to create a pillow cover or tiebacks for another set of curtains. If you chose a printed sheet, you can color copy it and use it as a matte for framing pictures or art.

Sheet sizes are fairly standard, so keep these measurements in mind when you're searching:

✔ Twin sheets: 66 x 96 inches

✔ Full sheets: 81 x 96 inches

✔ Queen sheets: 90 x 102 inches

✔ King sheets: 108 x 102 inches

If you read "Sizing up your fabric needs" earlier in this chapter, you can see that queen- and king-size sheets are almost twice the width of most home decorating fabrics, giving you a lot to work with. Sometimes a twin sheet cut in half to create two panels is enough to treat a small window.

Shop for sheets just as you would unroll a bolt of fabric at the store. For window treatments, take the flat sheet out of its packaging (or if you can't, borrow the display sample), walk over to a source of natural light, and see how much light spills through.

Depending on where you shop for them, sheets can give you a lot of bang for the buck, especially the larger-size sheets. Check out our measuring chapters (Chapters 6 and 11) to determine how much fabric you need. You can usually buy a very good quality king-size flat sheet for about $35 to $45, which you can use to create draperies for an average-size window with some fabric leftover. Also, look out for those seasonal white sales! You can find some great bargains. (See more info on finding cheap sheets in the "Fabric outlets" section earlier in this chapter.)

High-thread count designer sheets are also becoming more affordable, whereas they were once the privilege of the very rich. Why not consider using a sheet with a petite pattern and wonderful texture instead of fabric by the bolt? For a linen look, try an Egyptian cotton sheet. Egyptian cotton has beautiful draping qualities and works well for swag window treatments (see Chapter 7). For a tucked-and-pinned slipcover over that needs to fit over a hard-to-fit or unusually shaped sofa (see Chapter 12), look for sheets with a synthetic/cotton blend, or even an all-synthetic sheet. Though you may frown on sleeping on all-synthetic sheets, they may work well for you elsewhere in your home. In addition, blends and synthetics don't wrinkle as much.

Similarly, if you're creating a project that requires a slightly stiffer fabric, say, to hold pleats, as in our pleated draperies (or the London and Roman shades all in Chapter 16), very cheap sheets (those with poor fiber content and low thread counts) found at a bargain store work well. Their fiber content doesn't make them comfortable to sleep on, but their stiff texture may be just what you're looking for. These same sheets aren't durable enough for slipcover use because they're just too poorly made.

Pretreating: A Must for Happy Fabrics

Pretreating fabric (sometimes called prewashing or preshrinking) is simply exposing a sample of your fabric to water before you begin cutting and sewing it as a way of seeing how your fabric will react. Pretreating helps you decide if your fabric will be washable or if you'll need to dry-clean it.

A fabric is only as good as the extent to which it's prepared for use. Washing is a necessity, because doing so tells you a great deal about the fabric's characteristics. Washing a fabric answers these questions:

- ✔ Does it wrinkle or pucker?
- ✔ Do the colors run (is it *colorfast*)?
- ✔ Is there significant shrinkage?

Finding the answers to these questions is important before you begin measuring and cutting.

In this section, we discuss how to fight against frayed edges, the right temperatures in which to wash your fabrics, and why drying and ironing your fabric before you sew are important steps.

Coauthor Mark Montano firmly believes that you can find out almost everything you need to know about a fabric just by washing it. Simply wash a piece of the fabric before you commit to washing the total yardage. Washing fabric beforehand

- ✔ May change the fabric's finish
- ✔ May remove a shine that you would rather keep as a special element of the fabric's design
- ✔ May loosen decorative threads
- ✔ May cause colors to run, even though you used cold water

Most fabrics that say "dry-clean only" can become washable. You have to decide if the change or changes that take place during washing are acceptable to you, in exchange for the freedom of being able to launder. If not, you need to commit to spot-cleaning and/or dry-cleaning your creation.

Sometimes you'll be working with fabrics that have already been pretreated and sewn, such as ones mentioned in the easy window treatment projects in Chapter 7. You don't need to wash this fabric. Just care for it according to the label instructions.

Fighting fraying

Fraying happens when your fabric has cut edges, which is standard with any fabric that you buy off the bolt. After you've tested your fabric sample with water and determined that you intend to wash it, sew the cut edges on your sewing machine with a zigzag stitch, or serge (overcast) the cut edges with a serger. (You can also do this to fabric that you intend to dry-clean, but it's not strictly necessary.)

In addition, if you think your fabric runs the risk of fraying during the wash (or you've intentionally bought a fabric for its fraying qualities; see Chapter 7), treat it gently the first time out by:

- ✔ Washing it in its proper temperature but using the gentle cycle
- ✔ Washing it by hand in your bathtub in cool water
- ✔ Air-drying your fabric (see the section "Laundering your cherished creations" later in the chapter)

For small areas that show a bit of wear and tear, such as fragile seam areas, lace edges, or even an area where your scissors clipped a bit of fabric unintentionally, antifraying fabric sealant, like Fray Check, is a wonderful product. Apply the sealant with a little brush along the rough edges of the fabric after washing and air-drying to prevent fraying. For more information about fraying and applying Fray Check, see Chapter 5.

Washing and drying your fabric

The first thing you do when pretreating your fabric is wash it. Washing your fabric before sewing is important for a couple of reasons:

- ✔ **You test the fabric's colorfastness.** *Colorfastness* is simply how well your fabric holds its colors, and whether they bleed onto one another. Testing for colorfastness is important — and easy. Cut a small piece of fabric when testing. You may even want to try to wash it with an old white sock to see if any of the color transfers. If your fabric bleeds color onto the sock, or the colors have bled onto the background of the fabric, you'll have to commit to dry-cleaning it.

✔ **You preshrink the material.** Your fabric *will* shrink, and it's much better for it to shrink now rather than when you've finished your creation.

Don't forget to allow for some initial shrinkage when calculating how much fabric to buy. Half a yard or so extra is almost always plenty for a smaller project, like an ottoman or stool; opt for 3 yards for a larger project, like a sofa slipcover or long drapery.

Regarding the water temperature to use when pretreating your fabric, the old English expression, "Begin as you plan to go on" applies in situations. Always wash your fabric the way you plan to continue to wash it in the future. Check the information on the fabric bolt or cylinder tag and note the percentages of cotton, polyester, spandex, and the like, and the manufacturer's recommendations for washing. Write it down in your color notebook (see Chapter 2 for more about staying organized with notebook) if you don't think you can remember. Then if your fabric needs to be washed in cold water only, wash it in cold water during pretreating. If it says you can use lukewarm warm water, then use warm water the first time.

Always use cold water when you wash washable silks and other delicate fabrics.

After you've washed your fabric, you obviously want to let it dry completely. However, hot air is an insult to many fabrics and it's a culprit in puckering, shrinking, and thread damage. Some fabrics are dryer friendly, like all-cotton denims, but others need more time to rid themselves of moisture. Treat your fabric respectfully; don't just throw it in the dryer on high heat just to get the job done quickly. Instead, let it air-dry.

You probably have an "air-only" or "no heat" setting on your dryer, which means that the dryer only uses air, and no heat, in the drying process. This setting is fine for most fabrics to dry during the pretreating stage.

Ironing before you sew

Don't forget to press your fabric with an iron after the fabric is dry. Only after a good pressing is fabric truly ready for sewing.

Some fabrics still retain their *bolt wrinkles* or slight lines they acquired from staying on the bolt for a while. If they're still present after you've pretreated the fabric, you may want to use a *press cloth* to make them disappear.

When choosing a press cloth, make sure it's light colored to prevent color transfer, thin so the heat can penetrate to the fabric beneath, and smooth so no bumps or knobs in the press cloth will mar the fabric beneath. When you're ready to begin ironing, follow these three easy steps:

1. **Place the press cloth over your fabric.**
2. **Lightly spray it with water from a fine-mist spray bottle.**
3. **Iron with even strokes.**

You can use many items around the house for a press cloth. A soft thin white washcloth may work. Mark's favorite material for a press cloth is a scrap of clean, thin, white cotton flannel. Some people swear by old cloth diapers.

Caring for Your Finished Products

Treat your finished product as well as you did when it was still a pile of humble cloth. This section provides a few tips on washing, drying, adding fabric protectants, and more, all to extend the life of your window treatments and slipcovers.

Laundering your cherished creations

You probably need to launder your slipcovers more than your window treatments, but we recommend you launder your draperies and curtains at least once a year. Even if you can't see it, dust, cobwebs, and grime do build up, especially on the sides facing the street. If you want your beautiful creations to last and last, don't toss them in the washing machine and fill it up with hot water or throw them in the dryer on high heat. Instead, wash them in the washing machine under the gentle cycle or launder them by hand in the bathtub.

Air drying helps with the longevity of your fabrics, and if you've used any type of iron-on bonding tape like Stitch Witchery (see Chapter 5), air-drying helps it stay in its place.

You can air-dry one of two ways:

- ✔ Hang your creation up to let the water evaporate naturally over time. Inside or outside, it doesn't matter, unless you've chosen a fabric that will be hurt by the sun. If so, dry inside.
- ✔ Use the "air-only" or "no heat" setting on your clothes dryer.

Out, damned spot! Out, I say

Perhaps if Lady Macbeth would have known about spot-cleaning, she might not have been so upset. You don't have to worry though. If you have a small stain on your window treatment or slipcover, and you don't really want to wash the whole item, you can spot-clean it.

To spot-clean, you can either use a dry-cleaning solution or a very mild, nonperfumed soap or Woolite and water. The best way to spot-clean is to first try your cleaning method on a hidden area of your fabric — say, on a hem that doesn't show — and then if the fabric doesn't change or isn't damaged by the spot-cleaning, go after the stain.

If you discover that your attempt at spot-cleaning is worse than the stain itself, take it in to a professional.

If your window treatment fabric isn't a specialty fabric (by that, we mean it's a nonembellished one), or your slipcovers are made from a sturdy, unadorned fabric, by all means, use the air-only setting. If you have any doubts about the ability of your creation to stand up to the clanging and banging inside a metal tube, hang it on the line.

Scotchgarding against stains

Some home-decorating fabrics already come with stain-repellent surfaces. If your fabric doesn't, though, you may want to consider trying Scotchgard. This product repels dirt and spills, and it's especially great at keeping dry-clean–only fabrics free of stains to avoid a costly trip to the cleaners. Scotchgard also makes a cleaner that gently foams away stains, while at the same time leaving behind a coating of Scotchgard antisoiling agent.

Apply Scotchgard to your finished slipcover or window treatment after it's sewn and the trim is on. Follow the instructions on the can and make sure to test a small, inconspicuous piece of fabric, as well as any trim you plan to attach, for colorfastness and to see if the fabric's texture changes (stiffness may be a problem) before you spray the entire piece. If you launder your creation, use more Scotchgard to replace what rinsed off in the washing machine.

When using any Scotchgard product, be sure to work in a well-ventilated area, preferably outside; the fumes can be mighty strong! If you have any chemically sensitive individuals in your house, you may want to avoid using it.

Working with dry-clean–only fabrics

Before you commit to dry-clean–only fabric for a window treatment or slipcover, take a long, hard look at your willingness to commit to the time, energy, and money that's needed to maintain them. Yes, they're beautiful, but only if they're well cared for.

Don't be shy about accepting that pretty fabric from your grandma or great-aunt. Home dry-cleaning solutions can help! These solutions are now available over the counter. Now you can use them in your dryer, saving time and money. They're a nice choice especially for not-heavily soiled fabric that you like, but which has a peculiar odor. They remove odors, such as tobacco smoke, mothballs, and cooking stenches, and impart a nice smell.

A spot-cleaning solution is also available to apply directly to a specific stain, in case you've bought a slightly damaged or dirty remnant or discounted bolt of fabric. Always test a swatch before applying it. Another benefit is that these home kits work to remove wrinkles from fabric.

Be careful when you use dry-cleaning solution on chintzes and sateens, because it may take away the coveted sheen of some fabrics. Remember to always test a dry-cleaning solution and its results on an extra piece of fabric.

Note: If you have a stain on one window panel of fabric, you need to take both panels to the drycleaners. If not, the dry-cleaned panel will have a slightly different look than the nontreated one. The same goes for using dry-clean–only fabric for a slipcover: If you're dry-cleaning a matching pillow, consider cleaning the whole slipcover too, if you're a stickler for matching.

Chapter 4

Latching On to Hardware

. . . .

. . . .

*W*hen making window treatments and slipcovers, choosing the right hardware can make or break your project. Imagine your room as a giant body that needs dressing. Hardware makes everything "hang right," while elaborating on your style and making your project really shine.

This chapter helps you begin to think about the right hardware for your window treatments and your slipcovers without breaking the bank. We discuss some of the best hardware choices as well as how and where to incorporate them to get the look you want — and need.

Why Choosing Hardware Early On Matters

For window treatments, your first decision is whether you want a hardware style that is part of the room's overall look, or one that is hidden away. This decision partly informs what type of treatment you'll choose and how it will be constructed. Your second decision is where to mount your rod, because you use that information, along with the size of any rings or clips, to measure your treatment length. For more, see Chapter 6.

Keep these few points in mind regarding window-treatment hardware:

  ✔ When rods, poles, brackets, finials, holdbacks, and rings are part of the window design, you want to match them to one another. They also must complement your room's other decor elements (such as the color scheme and style of your rugs, furniture, doorknobs, drawer pulls, and so on) and to any existing architectural elements in the room (such as friezes, ceiling trims, wainscoting, and so on).

✔ The position of your tieback or holdback creates a specific look and determines how much light and air enter your room.

Honing In on Hardware for Your Window Treatments

Mounting hardware isn't an afterthought of window design, but rather an integral part of your window treatment and another decorative element with which you can create your final look. For example, if you have your heart set on tab curtains (see Chapter 15), you need to plan for the right kind of rod to use at the same time you're thinking of your treatment, because the rod will show and become part of the overall look. For a swag-style treatment (see Chapters 7 and 15), much of your pole will show as well.

You also need to consider whether your window treatment has to move or not. Are you treating a wide bank of windows that you want fully exposed by day? You can consider a metal pole with metal rings for easy movement. For a small window whose one-panel fabric treatment can be easily pushed back, try a swag holder mounted on one side.

Our favorite places for picking up curtain rods and poles are at church bazaars, garage sales, flea markets, and thrift shops. Keep the dimensions of poles and rods that you need handy in your color notebook (see Chapter 1 and 2) or a blank notebook, along with a miniature tape measure. Pick them up cheap, bring them home, and paint or stain them. You can even wrap them with fabric, and you've picked up your hardware for a song.

Knowing the basic components of mounting hardware

The following list includes some of the most common components of mounting hardware for window treatments:

✔ **Rods or poles:** You use either a rod or a pole to hang most window treatments.

  • *Rods* are made of plastic or metal and usually are adjustable, and they come in many different finishes including brass, gold tone, brushed metal, wrought iron, and polished metal. They come in many shapes: fluted, twisted, rounded, square, and many more.

- *Poles,* on the other hand, are usually made of wood, bamboo, plastic, or metal, but aren't adjustable. Wooden poles come in many types. Pine and birch are the most common types, and you can usually paint or stain them if they're untreated.

✔ **Brackets:** *Brackets* are the supportive holders that keep rods and all poles in place. They can mount onto walls, window frames, or even ceilings. Some brackets are purely functional, while others have a decorative life all their own. Most *inside-mount rods* (rods that mount inside the window frame, such as tension rods) don't need brackets, so this piece of hardware isn't always necessary. (Check out "Deciding where to place it" later in this chapter for more on inside-mount and outside-mount rods.)

✔ **Finials:** *Finials* are the end accessories that you add after the rod or pole has slid into the two brackets and is in its proper place. Finials are both decorative and functional; they're attractive and keep curtain rings from sliding off the rod or pole. (Again, inside-mount rods don't use finials.)

If you're working with an outside-mount rod and you decide on ornate brackets, let your finials match their style exactly, or else let the bracket shine. You don't want too many clashing styles to distract from your window treatment.

✔ **Rings or clips:** The last element to add is rings or clips that attach to the fabric at the top of your treatment and go over your rod or pole.

- *Curtain rings* have smaller rings at the bottom (where you can sew your curtain ring to your fabric or add a small hook) or tiny internal clips (for grabbing onto the fabric). They come in many finishes to complement your other hardware elements.

- *Cafe clips,* sometimes called rings with clips in this book, have tiny clips at the bottom that are often disguised by a pretty decorative motif, such as leaves, stars, or other shapes.

Many housewares stores that sell hardware carry rods, brackets, and finials in sets, but you can still mix and match if you want. Buying the sets takes most of the guesswork out of hardware, but doesn't allow for a lot of creativity. If you choose to mix and match, be sure everything works together and complements each other. Test your rings to ensure they fit over your pole or rod and check that your finials fit your pole or rod. Also check to see if your choice of mounting hardware complements a dominant motif of your room or window treatment. For example, if your damask fabric features a scroll design, see if you can find a wood or iron bracket that has a similar scroll design. Just remember: Your hardware elements need to look great *and* fit great together.

Counting your clips and rings

A variety of curtain-hanging devices are available, and the many clips and rings all have different qualities. Think about how you'll hang your treatment concurrent with its construction and you'll pick the right ones.

✔ **Style:** When choosing curtain clips, look for something that matches your window treatment. Curtain clips come in a few styles made from many materials, including wood, plastic, and metal, some of which you can further customize with paint.

For instance, are you looking for a charming, rustic look? A dark wood may work. A modern, streamlined treatment? Chrome metal's your ticket. Something romantic and slightly baroque? Perhaps a shabby chic-style, cracked white-paint clip.

✔ **Size:** Clips and rings also come in a few different sizes. Bear in mind that your clips and rings have to fit *over* your curtain rod, so buying them both at the same time is a good idea. (Doing so usually isn't a problem, because they're usually sold right next to each other in sewing supply stores.) If you can, test them right on the rod before you buy. Check how well they glide across the rod you've chosen.

We're not advocating that you break into the sealed plastic bags the clips come in, but perhaps you can ask a salesperson if you can see a floor sample.

✔ **Weight:** Another thing to keep in mind: Are the clips you fancy strong enough to support the weight of the fabric you've chosen for a particular project? If your fabric is heavyweight, make sure your clips are too.

Figure 4-1 shows a few basic rings to consider.

Figure 4-1:
Rings to
consider.

Clip rings   Rings with eyes   Rings with clips

Choosing a rod that works with your treatment

Before you choose your rod or pole, you need to decide if you want a treatment that features the rod or pole as a design element, or if you want your rod or pole to be purely functional and not visible.

The rods and poles that "show" are

- ✔ All manners of metal, wood, and plastic rods and poles with coordinating finials, brackets, holdbacks, and rings, in styles ranging from historical reproductions to traditional to modern are decorative
- ✔ Specialty rods, such as swivel rods that swing out, which are useful in treating inward-opening casement windows, doors, and doorways, and cafe rods, used for cafe curtains
- ✔ Swag holders, which are also decorative, and can be used either to mount swag treatments or used in place of holdbacks

The rods and poles that "hide" are

- ✔ Flat rods
- ✔ Sash rods
- ✔ Tension rods

Sometimes these nondecorative rods are round, sometimes they're flat, sometimes they're opaque (usually white or off-white), and sometimes they're clear. Most rods attach with brackets, but you can also find magnetic-backed rods to use on metal window frames or doors.

After you've decided on your style, consider your rod or pole's functionality. If you're creating draperies in velvet or brocade, your rod or pole must be strong enough to hold a medium- to heavyweight fabric. Additionally, remember that the pole or rod needs to "match" your fabric on an aesthetic level; if you're using a lightweight fabric to create an informal-looking treatment, you don't want a rod or pole that overwhelms your fabric by being too thick, heavy, or formal.

Basic rods for traditional windows and treatments

If you're creating a traditional treatment for a regular window — a simple double-hung window or a casement window — these rods will do the trick.

- ✔ **Cafe rods:** These rounded metal tubes mount with U-shaped brackets and usually are capped with small metal finials on the ends. You can use them for the cafe curtains in Chapter 14 or any type of curtain that gathers directly onto the rod. You can also use them with curtain rings or cafe clips.

- ✔ **Flat rods:** These lightweight rods are called "flat" rods because they're not rounded like most rods. They're great for mounting any treatment with a rod sleeve, such as valances. Flat rods come in 1-inch, 2½-inch, and 4½-inch widths. They snap onto metal curtain rod brackets (which are nondecorative) that are mounted with screws to the wall or window frame, depending on how far you want your treatment to extend.

Wide flat rods are just like flat rods, but they jut out from the wall 2½ to 4½ inches, providing drama and room underneath for hanging another type of drapery. (Check out our description of crisscross curtains in Chapter 14 for a dual application of two flat rods, which you can also create with two wide flat rods.) Wide flat rods are made of metal or clear plastic. The clear plastic is useful when you're using a sheer-fabric window treatment. They snap onto metal curtain rod brackets (which are nondecorative) that are mounted with screws.

✔ **Sash rods:** These curtain rods attach to the window's sash with little brackets that secure them in place. You can use them for the casement curtains project in Chapter 14 or whenever you're treating French doors.

✔ **Tension rods:** These rods come equipped with spring mechanisms inside and little rubber tips on the ends. They're adjustable and slide in and expand to mount inside your window, and thus don't need brackets, saving your frame a lot of abuse. Use them when you want to show off beautiful wood frames. They're also great when you want to show off a special-shape window, such as a Palladian-style window, whose frames you don't want to cover with extra fabric. Tension rods are best used with lightweight fabric curtains because they rely on a spring-loaded mechanism, not a bracket, to keep them in place.

Specialty rods for unusual windows and treatments

Some windows are unusually shaped, and some window treatments use a lot of fabric; both design scenarios would benefit from specialty rods.

✔ **Arched window rods:** These rods are rounded so you can mount them flush to the arch of a Palladian window or other round-type window. (A *Palladian window* is a three-paneled wall of windows — the center window is topped with an arch, and the two outside windows are shorter and have a square top; see our discussion in Chapter 6 on unusual window types.) They're usually clear so you can work with sheer fabrics, allowing the sunshine in.

✔ **Bay window rods:** Try these specially made rods, which consist of three pieces of metal that can be adjusted to mount at the proper angle over the three windows that traditionally comprise bay windows.

Not all ceilings, window moldings, or floors are completely square. In order for your treatment's fabric to drape evenly, you have to ensure that your rod is mounted level and not slanted. Get out your trusty L-square to verify that your rod or pole is mounted straight.

✔ **Traverse rods:** Traverse rods are a little more complicated than the others mentioned in this list. They're great for longer, heavier draperies that can't conveniently be pulled open and closed by hand. If you're using a heavyweight fabric, a traverse rod may be the right one for you. Because these heavyweight draperies have more fabric, traverse rods need more support. In addition to end brackets, you may want to pick up some additional support brackets, especially if your window requires a longer traverse rod. You can mount these additional supports every 2 feet or so.

This type of rod is less popular today, because window treatments tend to be less ornate, but it still has its good points. A traverse rod enables you to open and close your draperies by pulling a cord that moves slides along a track that you use to clip or hook your treatment's fabric right onto the rod. You can get the conventional type that are concealed when the drapery is closed or the decorative type that shows when the drapery is open or closed. Some traverse rods open in the middle of the window, and some open side to side (to the left or right).

✔ **U-shaped rods:** These steel rods are in the shape of the letter U that you can anchor to the wall above your bed to create a canopy treatment. With these rods you can introduce the softening magic of fabric to a room. Try a sheer fabric or match your fabric to your curtains or draperies.

Simple swag hardware

Hardware created especially for swags is often complicated; it includes wooden, fabric-covered mounting boards, rods with looped-on swag holding hooks (which look like the hooks with which faltering vaudevillians were hauled offstage), and other swag-specific devices. (In this book, however, we try to make your life a bit easier — by including swags that you merely hang or knot over the decorative rod of your choice and that you don't need all that costly, special hardware.)

Nevertheless, one item of swag hardware that you may want to consider is the swag holder. *Swag holders* mount to the upper left and right sides of your window frame. You then drape the fabric through the swag holders (the holder's decorative part covers the hole). Swag holders come in heart shapes, spirals, medallions, flower shapes, and many other configurations. If your fabric isn't too heavy, swag holders can replace a decorative rod and can support your swag treatment efficiently and elegantly. Match your swag holder style to your decor for a wonderful, cohesive effect. A variety of plastic swag holders are also available. They look like a circle with open segments. You simply pull the fabric through the self-covering segments and create the swag in the process.

Many knob-shaped metal holdbacks and swag holders are interchangeable, so don't limit your swag holder choices based on what their package calls them. Instead of draping the fabric through a hole, you loop the fabric around the projection arm of the holdback. Smaller loop-shaped holdbacks may work on swag treatments, too. Make sure you determine if your treatment features enough fabric to completely cover the nondecorative mounting area of the holdback.

Clueing in to curtain weights

Curtain weights can help all kinds of fabric treatments look better, but they're especially useful for lightweight fabrics that need a bit more weight to hang correctly. They come in a few different weights, and they're not just for curtains; you can use them to add a little heft to a dining chair slipcover, so the fabric on the bottom hangs well. They come in a few styles and are available at any fabric and crafts store (see our recommended resource list in Chapter 20).

Installing Window Hardware

Installing your window hardware the "right" way is a subjective concept indeed. So what's the only hard-and-fast law in installing the hardware? You need to install your hardware so that it doesn't come crashing down if you or a loved one pulls a bit too hard on the treatment. Otherwise how you hang your hardware is a matter of choice.

Deciding where to place it

When installing your window hardware, you first need to know whether the window hardware is *inside mount* or *outside mount*.

Inside mount

Inside-mount hardware consists of rod and brackets that sit within the frame of the window. They don't need finials because these rods are meant to disappear under the fabric of your treatment.

Choosing an inside mount for rooms such as foyers and half bathrooms can keep your treatment simple and doesn't overwhelm a small room. An inside mount also shows off special window frames by not obscuring them with fabric.

Inside-mount hardware is easy to figure out. In the case of tension rods, you can use one, which mounts at the top of the inside of your window, or you can use two rods for even more privacy: One mounts at the very top of the inside of your window, and the other mounts at the lowest part of the inside of your window. In the case of sash rods, they mount on the wooden or metal sash of the window.

The following are a few other instances where an inside mount may work:

✔ Corner windows, or a single window placed very close to a corner, work well with an inside-mounted tension rod.

✔ Architectural elements above windows or special-shaped windows, such as Palladian windows or arched windows, often need an inside mount to show them off.

Inside-mount hardware has its limitations because you must work within the window frame. Meanwhile, outside-mount hardware gives you more freedom. See the next section for more about outside-mount hardware.

Outside mount

Outside-mount hardware consists of a rod or pole, brackets, and finials that sit outside the frame of the window. You decide exactly where outside the frame: an inch above the top of the frame, 5 inches, or even a foot.

Different outside-mount hardware placements can help you achieve the following looks:

✔ You can create the illusion of height on a too-short window by mounting your rod 6 inches above your window frame and adding a long or floor-length treatment, which draws the eye up and down.

✔ You can create the illusion of width on a too-tall window by mounting your rod right above the window frame and adding a valance on a rod wider than the window width along the top of your window, which will draw the eye left and right.

✔ You can allow the maximum amount of light to come in by installing your rod or pole above the window frame and keeping your holdbacks or tiebacks higher than the midpoint of your window (see Figure 4-2).

✔ Instead of a curved rod, which usually has to be custom made, you can use a series of holdbacks or swag holders placed along the top curve of an arched or half-circle window. Loop the fabric around the swag holders, letting the ends drape down the sides. Doing so highlights the window's special shape.

✔ You can consider mounting your rod on the ceiling if the space between the top of your window frame and the ceiling is limited. Use special brackets that allow the rod to slide in securely and be sure to use the appropriate drywall anchors to ensure that the brackets stay firmly in place.

✔ You can plan on using asymmetry to create visual interest. By placing your tiebacks or holdbacks at different positions, you can create a few different silhouettes (see Figure 4-2).

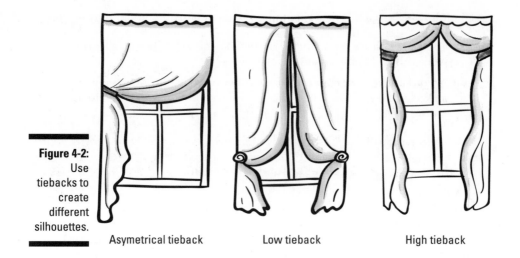

Figure 4-2:
Use
tiebacks to
create
different
silhouettes.

Asymetrical tieback   Low tieback   High tieback

How to mount your window hardware

Most hardware comes with mounting instructions from the manufacturer, but the following tips can also help you mount yours successfully:

- ✔ Measure down from the ceiling to where you intend to mount your hardware, because not all windows are plumb and level.

- ✔ Use a retractable steel measuring tape to ensure that all brackets are mounted at the same height.

- ✔ Keep an erasable pencil close by to mark where your brackets will mount.

- ✔ Install your hardware in the following order:

  For rods or poles used with rings, first the brackets go up and then the rings slide onto the poles or rods. Next insert the pole or rod into the brackets, and then cap the ends with the finials. Add your window treatment to the rings last. (If you're sewing your treatment fabric onto the rings with eyes, do your sewing before you add your rings to the pole or rod.)

  For rods or poles that go through a rod sleeve sewn along the treatment top, insert your rod or pole into the sleeve before putting the rod through the brackets, and then attach your finials, if needed.

- ✔ Use a stud finder to find the wall studs, which offer a safer anchor for holding hardware.

✔ If you're installing brackets into plaster or drywall, consider using *molly bolts,* which expand inside the wall, keeping all your hardware elements tightly in place.

✔ When installing into brick or concrete, purchase masonry bolts, which also expand.

✔ To mount a rod to the ceiling, measure out from the window frame and mark your bracket holes with your pencil. Be sure to use molly bolts to install your hardware safely and securely, because gravity will be working against your rod or pole.

✔ If your rod is extra-long, add a center bracket to keep the rod from sagging. Consider using an extra bracket, even if your rod is short, if you're making a treatment from heavy fabric.

✔ Above all, keep safety in mind. Be sure your ladder is secure. If you're mounting a heavy rod or pole, double-check that your brackets are securely fastened and can support your treatment's weight. If you have small children in the house, consider metal, wood, or plastic holdbacks or swag holders instead of fabric or rope-like tiebacks, so there's no chance of them pulling or swinging on looped fabric.

Utilizing Slipcover "Hardware"

Some individuals don't normally think of the words "slipcover" and "hardware" in the same sentence, but we think they do go together. In this section we suggest a few helpful "hardware" items that can make your slipcover stay in place and look better.

Using no-slip rubber

No-slip rubber is a type of open-weave rubber that grips flat smooth surfaces on both its sides. Although many people use no-slip rubber under area rugs, it can also keep fabric from slipping from fabric. No-slip rubber keeps a no-sew slipcover from sliding off when placed over uncovered cushions, and it also keeps slipcovered cushions from sliding off a slipcovered sofa, loveseat, or armchair. Try it between your dining room table and your tablecloth instead of a table pad.

No-slip rubber comes in rolls, can be cut with any type of scissors to measure at home, and is a great alternative to measuring, buying, cutting, and sewing cotton batting (the stuff traditionally applied to sofas and other furniture to keep slippage to a minimum).

Bed stays

Bed stays consist of a length of elastic with two fasteners at each end — usually snaps or clips — meant to attach to two pieces of fabric. These neat items are sold under many brand names, and they're traditionally used to keep bed sheets tucked in place.

However, why not use them to keep draped slipcover fabric from shifting? Attach one end to the inside of your slipcover, in the skirt area, or at the back of the slipcover, and the other to the underside of your furniture, or you can attach it from one part of the slipcover to another, for instance around the leg of a chair.

The joys of Velcro

Velcro consists of two interlocking sections that release with ease yet adhere extremely well. To our minds, it is the greatest stuff on earth! We recommend its use for our washing machine slipcover in Chapter 16. Many types of Velcro are available to suit many different types of projects. Choose a lighter Velcro for lightweight fabrics and heavy-duty Velcro for heavyweight fabrics. Heavy-duty Velcro lasts the longest and keeps everything in place the best.

You can apply Velcro anywhere that you want a bit of adhesion — in the tuck-in area of your sofa, on the sides of your ottoman, on the seatback of your dining room chair, and so forth. If you're covering an old piece of furniture that will always be covered, you can apply Velcro right to the old upholstery; just sew or adhere one side of the Velcro to the furniture and the other to the slipcover.

Though we like the kind of Velcro that you sew into place because it tends to be thinner and easier to handle, you can also buy the self-adhesive Velcro. It may be a bit bulkier, but it cuts your project-making time in half. Velcro is very inexpensive in all its forms; buy a few types and experiment if you want.

Upholstery locks

Upholstery locks look like tiny stainless-steel corkscrews with clear plastic lids. They're very useful in keeping draped fabric in its place. They twist into place and twist out when you want to change or launder your slipcover. Upholstery locks usually come in packs of 25, which is enough for a sofa plus two chairs.

The holes made by these tiny locks are very small, but they're holes nonetheless. These locks work the best on old furniture or furniture with fabric with a nap, like velvet or corduroy, into which tiny holes will disappear.

Chapter 5

Getting the Right Tools within Reach

In This Chapter

▶ Keeping the right tools close at hand

▶ Adding some cool accessories to your sewing arsenal

Your time is precious — particularly when you're sewing your window treatments and slipcovers, so why would you want to waste any of it? To make the most of your sewing hours, you need to obtain and maintain all the correct tools together in one place for easy access and use. And knowing all about those little sewing extras (clips, pins, weights, and measures) means, believe it or not, less time spent in front of the sewing machine or with a threaded needle in your hand.

In this chapter, we show you the tools of the trade that you'll be reaching for time and again, whenever the creative bug bites you. We show you exactly what you need to finish your projects quickly and effectively — the first time.

Identifying the Must-Haves in Your Sewing Tool Kit

In the world of design, you're only as good as your tools, so be sure to have top-notch gear. Gather your tools close by you as you work, check them frequently to make sure they're in top shape, and always store everything together (see Chapter 1 for more tips about gathering your supplies and creating a workspace). From scissors and measuring tapes to irons and sewing grids, in this section we provide a list of goods for you to keep on hand to get you through your projects.

Cutting to the core: Must-have shears

Cutting fabric is both an art and a science, and in the world of Seventh Avenue, New York City's fashion district (where coauthor Mark Montano worked for many years), the fabric cutter is a pro whose only job is cutting fast and cutting perfectly.

You don't have to be a pro to cut fabric well; you just need to remember two important points:

- ✔ Take your time when you cut.
- ✔ Be sure to have the right cutting tool.

Both can really help you avoid costly cutting mistakes.

We recommend that you have the following two types of cutting tools on hand (although you may want more):

- ✔ **Dressmaker's shears:** These special scissors have two different finger holes: One is round, and the other is oblong. The blades — one is bent at an angle and one is straight — are very sharp so you can easily push them through the fabric. The bent-angle blade, controlled by your thumb, provides a place along the straight blade for your index finger to rest during long bouts of cutting. The bend also prevents you from lifting the fabric off the table, making a more accurate cut easier to achieve.

   For your dressmaker's shears, we recommend Fiskars brand shears, which always are top-notch, precise, and simple to use. Fiskars also makes scissors for people who are left-handed.

- ✔ **Pinking shears:** This scissorlike device is great for cutting to prevent *fraying* (unwanted unraveled threads along fabric edges), which is especially important with such fabrics as cottons and linens (because they have looser weaves) and brocades. The edges that result from *pinking* (a zigzag cut) these kinds of fabric don't unravel, thus saving you time and money and preventing frustration.

Be sure to try a few different types of shears before you buy them. That way you can find the one that fits your hand the best.

You may also want to keep a pair of embroidery scissors around for light tasks, such as trimming stray threads, cutting small pieces of fabric, or cutting decorative trims. They're about 3 inches long and are perfect for getting into small areas and crevices.

Always keep your scissors sharp. Take them to your local sewing machine shop whenever you lose that beloved sliding feeling you get while cutting. Sharp scissors ensure that your cutting tasks are a breeze — but watch your fingers!

On pins and needles

To keep your fabric together, sometimes you need to grab pins of different varieties. Whether you're using a sewing machine or working by hand, here's the skinny on needles that you need to sew your project right.

Extralong straight pins

Extralong straight pins are a must for any sewing project, but they're especially important for use in draperies, curtains, and slipcovers, when you're using longer pieces of fabric that need the extra stability. We talk about using these pins extensively in Chapters 7 and 16, where we show you how to drape swags.

Some people swear by a pincushion to keep their straight pins handy. Cushions are convenient and easy, but you can't always determine the length of a pin that you're pulling out, which can get a bit annoying after a while if you're looking for an extralong pin. If you prefer, keep extralong straight pins close by in a dish or even better, a lidded box, and try a magnet to pick them up a few at a time (or all at a time if you drop the dish!).

Safety pins

One of the greatest inventions ever is the safety pin. Coauthor Mark is a big fan of using safety pins rather than straight pins for attaching fabric to patterns so the fabric doesn't slip, shift, or move. Safety pins not only keep fabric in place until you're ready to sew, but in some of the no-sew or low-sew projects in this book, they also replace sewing entirely. Check out Chapter 7, where we use 2-inch safety pins for *shirring* (gathering fabric to create a pleat) and in Chapter 9 for our shortcuts with window treatments.

Safety pins usually come in two basic colors: gold or brass tone, or silver or chrome tone. If you choose a project where you'll incorporate them into the curtain's design (like in Chapter 7), buy a fresh box and use only the pins from the new box, which give your project a more cohesive look. Believe it or not, not all safety pins are fashioned the same. They may look identical, but each company adds a slightly different spin.

You may need an array of sizes, so look for 1-inch-long, 2-inch-long, and 3-inch-long safety pins. They're cheap, and you can always find a use for them, even when you're not sewing.

The larger-size safety pins that some drycleaners use to attach garments to hangers can be very useful — save them and keep them handy.

Sewing machine needles

Most sewing machines can sew lightweight, silky fabrics for window treatments and heavy-duty fabrics for slipcovers. The trick is using the right needle.

- ✔ **Regular sewing machine needles:** *Regular* needles are used on lightweight or mediumweight fabric. Use size 9 or 10 for light fabrics, like voile, eyelet, crepe, batiste, light charmeuse, or any other lightweight fabrics listed in Chapter 2. Use size 11 or 12 for mediumweight fabrics like satin, medium Ultrasuede or other faux suedes, velour, velvet, and the like.

- ✔ **Heavy-duty sewing machine needles:** Quite a few of the projects in this book call for a heavy-duty needle. Be sure to use heavy-duty needles (and thread) when you're sewing heavier fabrics, such as brocades, heavy denims and ducks, vinyl, canvas, and upholstery fabric. These needles are usually numbered 14 and 16.

We recommend Singer needles for all your sewing needs, light, medium, and heavy. In coauthor Mark's experience, they last the longest and make the cleanest sewn line, but check the owner's manual of your sewing machine to be sure they're compatible.

When you're sewing, if your sewing needle skips or makes uneven stitches, change it. Keep plenty of sewing machine needles on hand, because you never know when you'll need a new one.

Measuring up: Essential measuring devices

You've probably heard the mantra of contractors and carpenters: "Measure twice, cut once." Well, people who sew need to adopt it as their favorite phrase, too. Measuring your fabric is important, and measuring accurately is essential. In this section we discuss some of the handy measuring tools you turn to time and time again.

Cloth tape measures

Cloth tape measures enable you to measure your fabric (and prevent frustration when determining your fabric's dimensions), check your measurements on patterns, and much more. A cloth tape measure also serves well when you're measuring a rounded sofa arm or back, because you need the flexibility to go around those curves.

Most cloth tape measures are 60 inches long, but some notions departments of fabric and crafts stores stock ones that measures 100 to 120 inches, which are useful for big projects. If you're having a hard time finding an extralong tape measure, though, simply create your own by taping two of the shorter cloth tapes together.

If your tape measure has seen better days and is starting to curl or doesn't stay put, try backing the metric side with some flexible heavy-duty tape. The backing straightens out the tape measure and gives it some weight, but you'll still be able to roll it up. (For all you Francophiles, or international readers, feel free to cover up the "inches" side.)

Don't use metal retractable tape measures for measuring fabric because they're unwieldy, they don't lie flat on the surface of the fabric, and they don't do curves well. However, metal tape measures are great for determining window dimensions.

Sewing grids

A *sewing grid* is a device that enables you to easily measure your fabric when it's spread out on a flat workspace. You can then cut it straight or at right angles. Being able to cut right angles is especially useful when creating panels, such as those that require a more precise measurement like casement curtains with panels that fit over rectangular windows (see Chapter 14).

You can buy sewing grids at any sewing store, or you can customize one yourself. After all, a sewing grid is just made out of paper.

To make your own sewing grid, follow these easy steps:

1. **Lay out and cut some butcher paper so that you'll have adequate width and length to cover the area you seek to measure.**

   Your grid needs to be slightly larger than the largest area you'll be measuring, say the back of a sofa or an extralong window.

   You can pick butcher paper up at any crafts store, where it comes in sheets or on a roll.

2. **Tape the paper down to your sewing table or other flat workspace.**

3. **Using a marker and a ruler, measure a grid in 5-x-5-inch squares.**

   Using larger squares helps you make larger patterns for draperies and slipcovers.

Other great measuring tools

Besides measuring tapes and sewing grids, you also can use the following tools:

- ✔ **L square (drafting square):** An L-square is, as you can imagine, shaped like the capital letter L, and is used for creating a perfect corner. You may want to keep an *L square* around if you decide to make patterns. Even if you aren't going to make a pattern, an L-square can help you keep any line straight and any corner square.

- ✔ **Seam gauge:** This 6-inch ruler with an adjustable slide that moves up and down its length is very helpful for measuring small and narrow areas of fabric, such as the long seams and hems typically found in window treatment panels. This device enables you to verify whether you've measured evenly, just by sliding the seam gauge along the hem.

- ✔ **Yardsticks:** A wooden, plastic, or metal yardstick (and even shorter rulers) is great when you need to draw straight lines on fabrics (using tailor's chalk, which we discuss in the next section). In fact, we recommend using yardsticks for a few projects in Chapters 14 and 15.

Making a mark and chalking it up

Don't be afraid to draw lines on your fabric! Creating lines on your fabric is often an essential step in getting a great fit. With the right tools the marks disappear, and only you'll know your creation once looked a bit like a county road map.

You also need a good way to mark up your patterns so that every line is clear and concise. Here's how:

- **Disappearing tailor's chalk:** Also referred to as dressmaker's chalk, this tool is essential for marking lines on your fabric. It washes off easily, leaving no trace. (Chapter 10 has a bit more info on using chalk when creating slipcovers.)

- **Washout pencils and markers:** Special marking pencils or pens that are made for fabric also are helpful when working on light fabrics, and they also wipe off well. Use them for marking where to sew rings with eyes directly onto a fabric panel, or where to sew a pleat.

- **Colored pencils:** Keep two different colored pencils around — one for drawing your pattern lines on your butcher paper, say black, and another color, say red, so you can cross out mistakes. That way when you're ready to cut, you always know which lines are correct.

If you're using an unusual piece of fabric (for instance, a piece of vintage fabric or a fabric from a far-off land, the fiber content of which you're not entirely sure about), you may want to test your chalk and/or washout marking pencil on a corner or scrap piece of the fabric, let it sit a minute, and then wipe it away. Although tailor's chalk and marking pencils are made for all fabrics, it's better to be safe than sorry.

Using thimbles

A few projects call for *hand tacking* (sewing small areas of fabric or trim by hand), for which you may want to consider picking up a few thimbles, unless you don't mind risking your fingertips. Thimbles may look old-fashioned, but they go a long way toward protecting your fingers when pushing a sharp needle through fabric.

Thimbles come in plastic and metal and in many sizes. You usually use a thimble on the middle finger of your dominant hand. Pick one that feels right to you and keep a few extras on hand (no pun intended). They're cheap and useful — the perfect combination!

Ripping it out

Sometimes you have to undo what you've done, and that's when a *seam ripper* comes in handy. This useful little device removes stitches easily. It has an upturned sharp end that looks like a little claw, which pulls the stitch up and away from your fabric, preventing any unwanted cuts or nicks.

When your seam ripper gets dull, throw it out and get a new one at a fabric store, because they can't be sharpened. You'll save money on fabric (and hours of frustration) when your seam ripper is in top ripping form.

Doing trial-runs with muslin

Muslin is a versatile, off-white, cotton fabric that comes in many different weights. Best of all, it's inexpensive so feel free to use it as a test fabric. You can match the weight of the more expensive fabric you're using on a given project with muslin of an equal weight, and then use the latter to practice on.

Whenever you're trying something new or slightly more challenging — perhaps a project from Chapter 17 — that you believe your skill level may not match, or you're unsure whether your fabric calculation or measurements are correct, you may want to try it out in muslin first. After getting the pattern right with the muslin, you'll feel more confident in your skills and won't end up wasting the real fabric. You can even keep the completed muslin version as a "pattern" to use to make future slipcovers. Check out more on muslin in Chapter 10.

Ironing out the details

"Press as you go" is something you'll hear in roundtable discussions at sewing classes, and with good reason. Ironing your seams after you sew them is an essential step. You need a good-quality iron, preferably one that makes steam. Steam is helpful when you want to seal your curtain pleats in place, for example, or when you're working with heavy-duty upholstery fabrics.

Make sure that your ironing board is at least standard size, or long enough to accommodate the fabric lengths of swags, other draperies, and slipcovers. (Those little mini-boards sure are cute and convenient, but save them for pressing your unmentionables.)

You also want to have a good press cloth in case your fabric is wrinkled from pretreating or from off-the-bolt wrinkles. See Chapter 3 for more on choosing a press cloth.

If you intend to use Stitch Witchery, or any kind of adhesive-backed decoration, keep an iron-cleaning solution around. (To find out more about Stitch Witchery, check out "Stuck on you: Using bonding tape" later in this chapter.) If you accidentally iron over the adhesive, it can stick to your iron. Trust us, you don't want to gum up the plate of your iron and then transfer that substance onto another piece of fabric (or a loved one's favorite shirt) when your iron gets hot. It pays to have a reliable cleaning solution around for when you may need it.

Zeroing In on Special Accessories

This section provides a few extra items to keep nearby. You're sure to use them at one time or another.

Stuck on you: Using bonding tape

For creating light window treatments that are more decorative than functional, we're fans of iron-on bonding tapes (like Stitch Witchery). These sewing-substitute adhesive tapes come in a roll. The tape is like iron-on glue that is activated by an iron's heat and is available at any crafts or sewing store. It comes in many widths, so match your bonding tape to its task. Choose 1-inch tape for hems and wider types for attaching appliqués, such as decorative bows and flowers, without pulling out the thread and needle to sew. You can also use it for attaching most trims.

Sorry, we can't recommend iron-on bonding tape to substitute for "real" sewing, like creating pleats in curtains. Nor can we vouch for its use in creating slipcovers! It just isn't tough enough to hold seams together that need to stand up to the rigors of the human body.

Saving time with a serger

A serger is a machine separate from your sewing machine that specializes in cutting and finishing the edges of fabric in one easy step. It makes precision cuts and then overcasts the cut edge with thread, so your fabric doesn't unravel. Although sergers are used mostly to finish knitted fabric, you can use a serger on many types of fabric. A serger is a great timesaver when you're making a project with many finished seams and hems.

Sergers can go from $350 to $500 new, but you can pick them up used for far less. If you sew frequently, a serger is a good investment.

You need to stock up on thread, because a serger can use from three to six spools of thread at a time, compared to a sewing machine that uses only one spool on the same project.

If you use iron-on bonding tape, make sure that you hand wash your creation. Sewing tape isn't as sturdy or long lasting as real sewing. If you find the hem is coming undone after laundering, simply reiron it or reapply some more bonding tape in the places that are starting to give.

Staying fray-free with sealant

Whenever we're working with fabric that becomes frayed, we use a product called Fray Check. You can pick it up at any crafts or sewing store. Fray Check is a sealant applied the same way as glue; it dries clear and stops fabrics from fraying (see our discussion about using lace in Chapter 7).

Unfortunately, Fray Check isn't perfect. It can wash out even with light repeated laundering, causing the fabric to become even more susceptible to fraying. Be proactive and keep the bottle after you've completed the project, in case you need to apply more.

Fray Check is best used in small applications, for example, to mend a snipped edge of fabric or a corner of fraying material, but not along an entire seam. You may want to consider finishing highly fraying fabric with a serger (see the sidebar "Saving time with a serger" earlier in this chapter).

Having glue gun fun

A *glue gun*, an electricity-powered hand-held device that delivers hot glue in a thin stream, can be your best friend in a tight spot. Hot glue seals fabric together in the same way that needle and thread do. It's durable enough for many window treatment projects, and for adding trim to both window treatments and some slipcovers.

You can pick up a glue gun at any crafts store or hardware store. Remember you get what you pay for so buy the best one you can afford: Better quality glue guns tend to be larger, so make sure it's comfortable in your hand before you buy it. Unfortunately, the cute, cheap mini-glue guns don't last as long and tend to leak glue a bit more than others. We talk a more about how to use hot glue in Chapter 8.

Adding a zipper foot to your sewing machine

A *zipper foot* is a sewing machine attachment that helps you sew in zippers. They're narrower than other types of sewing feet, so you can get closer to the zipper's teeth. A zipper foot has one *toe* (the part that helps guide and hold the fabric down) shaped like a flat little trowel. The zipper foot attachment comes standard with most sewing machines. If you don't like the plastic one that came with your machine, buy a zipper foot made of metal that fits on your machine. (You can buy them at any sewing store for around $20.) The added weight of a metal foot holds the fabric in place better, making sewing much easier.

For fabrics with rubber or plastic backings (such as vinyl, or for certain types of fabric used for weatherproofed curtain linings), you may want to locate a Teflon zipper foot. It has a Teflon layer adhered to the bottom that enables the fabric to glide smoothly over the *feeder* (which is that little part with teeth that pulls the fabric along).

Sewing machines: The old and new of it

Whether you use an old workhorse that was handed down from your mother (or grandmother) or you like the modern conveniences of a new sewing machine is really a matter of taste.

Older machines: If you've been using the same older-model machine for years and don't want to upgrade, we understand completely. Like a comfy old sweater that has seen better days, you're used to the feel of your sewing machine and don't want to replace it. And if your machine works well, why should you, right? The biggest problem with older sewing machines, however, and something for you who are considering buying a used machine need to know, is that most don't have a reverse. Being able to reverse the stitching makes sewing much easier, because as you can tack the ends of your seams, it keeps them in place without a hassle. All newer machines have a reverse mode. The upside of older sewing machines is that they have much more power than newer ones. So choosing between new and old can be a bit of a trade-off; only you can decide what's more important. The Kenmore, Singer, Viking, or Sears brands have endured through the years. Look for older machines at yard sales, flea markets, and thrift shops, where you can find a great older machine for as little as $20!

When considering a used sewing machine, make sure that the belt is in good condition and that it can be replaced easily. Sometimes finding replacement parts for older machines is difficult. Making sure that the machine's timing is set and running well also is important. Lousy timing is the coup de grace for a sewing machine. Just like with a used car, you need to take your potential sewing machine for a test run. Bring your own fabric, load in your own thread, plug it in, sit down, and check out all its parts, from top to bottom, before buying.

Newer machines: New machines have some really fantastic, fun sewing features that are very seductive to sewing aficionados. Most have embroidery capabilities for embellishing your creations and new decorative stitch styles, such as scalloping, diamonds, and checkerboards. They also have stretch-stitch capabilities, which is a way to stitch knitted fabric so that the thread doesn't pop or break when the fabric stretches. Newer machines can create buttonholes, too. As tempting as all these items are, they're not necessary to sew in a basic and easy way. You only need a straight-stitching machine to create the projects we offer in this book, but the little extra features a new machine provides are fun to have, especially if you want to use contrasting thread color for visual interest.

Part II
Window Treatments in a Snap

The 5th Wave

By Rich Tennant

"Okay, Ms. Dolan, look closely, take your time, and tell us when you think you can identify a way we can improve this window treatment."

In this part . . .

This part focuses exclusively on your windows and how you can make easy, beautiful window treatments that will be a focal point of your room's decor. We offer you plenty of planning, measuring, and sewing advice that can simplify your creative life. However, if you don't want to use a sewing machine (or can't even sew a stitch), we also show you a few no-sew and low-sew projects you can whip up in an afternoon.

This part also includes an extensive discussion of window treatment accessories and trimmings that add plenty of dazzle, plus a few timesaving shortcuts. We'd be remiss in our duties if we didn't offer you some great tips on righting whatever went wrong, so you can find a few quick fixes in this part, too.

Chapter 6

Measuring, Making Patterns, and Cutting Fabric for Your Windows

. . . .

In This Chapter

▶ Keeping form and function in mind

▶ Identifying the tools you need

▶ Introducing the different types of windows

▶ Measuring your windows the correct way

▶ Creating patterns for window treatments

▶ Figuring out how to cut

. . . .

Making window treatments that give your windows that "just right" professional look may seem like a big challenge. You may feel a bit overwhelmed. How can you possibly remember every consideration before you begin to sew? We know that making window treatments may feel like an intricate puzzle that needs solving. Take a deep breath though. In this chapter we help with one of the big puzzle pieces — correctly measuring your fabric, making the pattern, and cutting your fabric.

Each window treatment project in this book has specific measuring advice at its start. However, before you delve into those individual projects, this chapter gives you some helpful basic information about measuring. In this chapter, we show you everything you need to know, from assembling your tool kit, to figuring out a window's anatomy, to grasping the ins and outs of hands-on measuring, to making your own patterns, and finally to cutting your fabric properly.

Considering Form and Function

"Form and function" is a phrase thrown around a lot in the design world, but its meaning is pretty simple. *Form* is the way the treatment and the window underneath look; *function* is how the treatment helps the window do its job, or modifies the window's job. To get the most out of your windows, always keep in mind how they work and how they look while you're planning a winning treatment. The way you cover your window affects the way they function.

Measuring affords you the benefit of taking a close, long look at your windows' form and their components. To consider your windows' form, take down your old treatment, get up on the ladder, and take a gander at your windows, their trim molds, and frames. Are they made of beautiful wood that you want to show off and incorporate into your window design? You may want to keep the sill free of extra fabric, if you use your sills for display purposes, or if a beloved family pet frequently perches there. Or are your frames and sills less than perfect and you want to cover them up completely? Maybe your window frames are just a neutral space that you can cover or uncover.

When looking at function, consider whether your window's depth allows for an inside-mount window treatment. Do you have a window that opens in an inward fashion? Are there cranks or other operating devices that will get in the way of certain types of treatments? These details can help you determine what kind of treatment you need. Also, understanding how much coverage you need influences how you measure for fullness.

Keep in mind that it may be necessary to measure each individual window. Don't assume that a bank of three windows all contain identical measurements: One may be a half-inch or a full inch wider or narrower. For example, what if you're creating a treatment that perches on the inside of your window frame? (If you have decorative trims, such as the beveled wood ones found in older homes, you may decide on a treatment that shows them off, and your treatment may only be as wide as the outside of your window frame.) Even an extra inch can make a difference.

Determining the measurements of your finished treatment is just as important as having your window dimensions on hand. For example, your window may measure 30 x 80 inches, but you intend to mount your rod 4 inches above your window frame, and you also want your curtains to extend 3 inches on each side of your window frame. To keep all this information straight, add the information into your color notebook (where you keep your swatches and other info to help you visualize your creation; see Chapter 2) under the title "treatment dimensions."

Keeping your color notebook handy with its detailed notes can help you when you're shopping to "imagine" the finished piece before you sew it, and also in buying the correct amount of fabric. Being ready with the right information also can help you obtain good advice from salespeople.

Lining Up Your Measuring Tools

Having the right tools is essential. In Chapter 5, we give you a list of general tools to create the projects in this book. This section focuses on the tools you need to measure your windows properly and plan your treatments.

The following list includes the measuring tools you need to have on hand:

- **A flexible/cloth tape measure:** Use it for measuring fabric for swags (see Chapter 5 for more on this useful tool).
- **Pen and notebook or paper:** Use these tools to record the measurements (see Chapter 2 for the importance of keeping a notebook).
- **Steel measuring tape (the retractable type that curls up inside a box):** Use it for measuring your window from top to bottom, left to right.

Before you start measuring your window and getting the pattern ready for your dynamite window treatments, we need to cover a few definitions we use throughout the book. Okay, you probably know what "width" means, but we want to make sure everyone is on the same page concerning the following terms:

- **Circumference:** The measurement around the perimeter of a circle or half circle (as on an arched or round window pane)
- **Diameter:** The measurement across the center of a circle (as across a round window, or across a curtain ring)
- **Length:** The vertical measurement from top to bottom (as up and down on a window)
- **Width:** The horizontal measurement from left to right (as across a window)

Also note that when we refer to *curtains*, we're using the generic term for "window treatment." You could make most of the projects in this book that we call curtains as draperies; usually all you have to do is extend their length (see "Measuring your windows for length" in this chapter for more info).

Acquainting Yourself with Your Windows

Just like people, windows come in all shapes and sizes. Some of them are easy to treat, some of them more of a challenge. Although we use 30- x 60-inch double-hung–type windows as the template for the projects in Chapters 7, 14, and 15 (for two reasons: it's a very common window size, and they're the size of the windows in Mark's New York City apartment), you need to remember that there is no such thing as a standard-size window.

In this section we look at the different types of windows you may encounter and then delve further into your windows to discover their different parts.

Identifying different types of windows

Before you start to measure your windows, you need to know what type of windows you have. This section addresses the most common type of rectangular windows as well as the most challenging types.

First, the most common:

- **Casement windows:** These windows have two vertical panes hinged at the sides that open inward or outward from the middle of the window with the help of handles at the bottom.

- **Double-hung windows:** These windows feature two horizontal panels, one of which slides up with the help of a sash to allow fresh air to enter through the bottom section.

- **Jalousie windows:** These windows open outward in three or four horizontal sections with the use of a crank.

Meanwhile, these windows may be the most challenging to treat:

- **Arched windows:** Windows whose tops are shaped like an arch, either alone or above another type of window.

- **Bay windows:** A bank of three flush double-hung windows similar to a Palladian window, but the panes are set at an angle and curve outward to create an alcove, or bay.

- **Cathedral windows:** A bank of windows, one of which is a stationary pane topped by a triangular or trapezoidal window, and flanked on either side by double-hung or casement windows.

- **Dormer windows:** These windows are recessed, usually by sloped ceilings on either side, as in attics.

- **Palladian windows:** A bank of three windows with an arch over the center window, or a similar variation.

- **Picture window:** This wide window has one large pane in the middle that doesn't open, flanked by two slimmer panels that are basically mini-double-hung windows or mini-casement windows.

- **Other odd-shaped windows:** They include everything from ovals, triangles, trapezoids, diamonds, very long and skinny windows, and very wide and short windows, some of which are stationary and decorative, and some of which open like double-hung windows.

Dissecting a window

Don't worry, this section isn't nearly as tough as biology class, but you do need to know a bit of anatomy so you can measure correctly. Following are the basic parts of a window:

- ✔ **Apron:** The piece of decorative wood underneath the windowsill. If the window doesn't have a windowsill, the apron looks like a continuation of the trim mold.

- ✔ **Frame:** Sometimes referred to as the *casing,* it's the inner, functional (mechanical) border of the window, usually made of metal.

- ✔ **Trim mold:** The area that trims the outside of the window frame, decorative in nature and usually made of wood. The trim mold lines the top, left, and right sides of the window frame.

- ✔ **Windowsill:** The area just below the bottom trim mold, which extends out to create a miniature shelf under the window.

Figure 6-1 illustrates these parts.

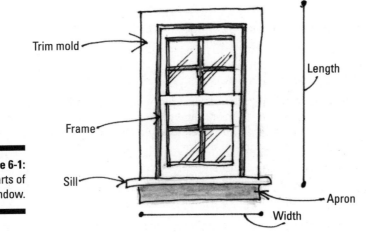

Figure 6-1:
The parts of
a window.

Consider taking a digital photo of your undressed window, enlarging it, and printing out a few copies. Label all the elements of your window using Figure 6-1 as a guide, noting how the window opens. You can then sketch over the photo, using it as a template for designing your window treatment.

Looking Closer at a Window's Measurements

You basically can choose from two types of window measurements: those for an outside mount (treatments whose width and length measurements extend past the window frames), and those for an inside mount(treatments whose width measurements remain inside the frames and whose length measurements usually extend to the top of the sill). We distinguish them in the following list:

- **Window width, for inside mount:** The distance between one side of the window to the other, measured from the outer edge of the frame to the other outer edge of the frame.

- **Window width, for outside mount:** The distance from the outside edge of the trim mold to the other. Adding inches to account for returns on either side increases the width measurement.

- **Window length, for inside mount:** The distance between the top of the window frame to the windowsill.

- **Window length, for outside mount:** The distance from the outside edge of the trim mold to the bottom of the window's apron.

- **Left and right returns:** The *returns* are the areas on either side of a flat rod that extend out so the treatment sticks out and away from the window. You may need to add a left or right return measurement when using flat rods that extend many inches out from the window.

- **Above and below the window:** Above is the distance from the top of the trim mold to the ceiling, and below is the area between the edges of the windowsill to the floor.

Getting the Gist of Measuring

Measuring your windows to figure out the finished width and length is simple. Keep the information in this section in mind before you begin measuring your windows.

Mounting your rod first for better measuring

After you decide on your style but before you begin to measure your window to decide how much fabric you need, mount your rod or pole. Or for outside-mount shade projects, mark the spot where you plan to place your mounting board (see the shade projects in Chapter 15 to read all about mounting boards). Having your hardware in place makes everything easier. You have a definite focal point and measuring aid in place. Check out Chapter 4 to help you decide how and where to install your hardware.

Also, for draping projects, likes draped swags (see Chapter 7), you need a rod or pole in place to test this treatment style and get the feel of how to drape fabric well. Mount your rod or pole and throw a silky type fabric you have at home over it to approximate what your treatment will look like. If you have a hard time visualizing whether a swag will fit your room, you can practice creating swags to see if it's a style you really like.

As you decide where to mount your hardware, keep these questions in mind:

- ✔ **How much light do you want to block out?** The more coverage you have on either side of your window, and above and below it, will obviously block more light; mount your rod accordingly.

- ✔ **How much privacy do you want the treatment to give?** Your fabric choice plays a big factor with privacy, but your hardware placement also plays a role. The more fabric coverage and the more your hardware extends on either side of your window, the more privacy you have.

- ✔ **How keen are you on creating the illusion of window height?** A rod mounted 6 inches above your window frame makes your windows appear longer and changes the room's proportion. You can even mount your rod on the ceiling for some treatments. See Chapter 4, as well as Chapters 8 and 9, for more illusion-creating tips.

Measuring your windows for width, using outside-mount measuring

Measuring your windows for curtains and draperies that hang outside the window molding is easy. Just decide how much coverage you want and mount your rod. Measure your rod from end to end. If you're using a flat rod that sticks out from the window more than an inch or so, take into account the return areas on the left and right sides.

Your width measurement also needs to consider the hem allowance for either side of each panel you're creating. *Hem allowance* is the allotted fabric needed to create a hem. It's usually double; for a ½-inch seam, allow a 1-inch measure. (We talk about specific seam allowance amounts in each project.)

Measuring your windows for width, using inside-mount measuring

Some treatments fit inside the window frame. For shades, measure from frame to frame. Not all windows are plumb, so take the width measurement in two or three places. Working with the smallest width figure, round up to the nearest quarter inch.

Determining cut panel width

To figure out the cut width of a flat-panel curtain or drapery (ones that aren't gathered at the top, such as pleated curtains), measure the window width and add 2 inches (one inch to each side) to allow for finishing the side hems.

For gathered curtains, add anywhere from 1½ to 2 times the width so that it has adequate fullness. Add seam allowance if you need more than one width of fabric for each panel.

For a lined flat panel, only add a half-inch on each side for finishing the sides. You don't need much extra fabric because it tucks inside.

When working with sheer fabrics, double the width measurement of each panel for adequate fullness. For heavier fabrics, use only 1½ times the fabric. Don't forget to add in your half-inch seam allowance!

Measuring your windows for length

When measuring your window for length, you need to keep two factors in mind: where you want your treatment to begin and end and the type of treatment you're making.

The following information on treatment types can help when you're measuring for length.

✔ Generally, *curtains* are treatments that extend from the top of the rod or pole to the top of the sill. Measure your length accordingly.

✔ *Draperies* are treatments that extend from the rod to any area below the sill (the beginning of the apron), usually to midapron and to the floor. For draperies, measure from the top of the rod to the midapron, or to a ½-inch above the floor, depending on the style you seek. To create puddles, add an extra 6 or 8 inches. Remember that draperies can be almost any length, so you need to decide how long you want them.

Keep in mind the opening mechanism of the window when deciding on treatment length. If your window opens inward, a treatment that extends past the sill may be difficult to manage.

✔ For the London and Roman shade projects in this book in Chapter 15, measure from the top of the mounting board, which goes above the window frame, to the top of the windowsill.

✔ For treating eaves and doorways, measure from the top of the rod (usually a tension rod that sits within an inch of the top of the doorway) to a ½-inch above the floor.

Determining cut panel length

To figure out a treatment's cut length, take the measured panel length and add an additional amount for the *rod sleeve* (the sleeve where the rod goes), if your treatment has one. If not, you need to account for the length of your curtain rings, and also add the correct amount for the bottom hem. Check out the next section for adding rod sleeves or curtain rings.

Adding a rod sleeves or curtain rings

To determine your rod sleeve's measurement, measure your rod's circumference and add 1 inch or 1½ inches; this extra ease allows fabric to hang properly and move across your rod easily.

The thicker your rod or pole, the more generous you need to be with your rod sleeve circumference. Also keep in mind the *backing* (underside) texture of your fabric type. Is it a napped or "sticky" type of fabric that doesn't slide easily; is it a silky or sheer fabric that does?

When planning your rod sleeve or curtain rings, keep these general guidelines in mind:

✔ For a tension rod, add 2½ to 3½ inches to your rod circumference.

✔ For a decorative pole, which is usually thicker, add 3½ to 4½ inches to your rod circumference.

✔ For small, thin rods that are used to hang more delicate curtains, such as casement rods or cafe curtain rods, add 1½ to 2 inches for your rod sleeve.

✔ For a treatment that uses curtain rings with clips, the general rule is to subtract 1½ inches for them (because it doesn't have a rod sleeve). If you're using outsized or custom-made rings, measure them and subtract the inches they'll take up. For a curtain ring that you sew on, subtract the clip's total diameter measurement from your length measurement. For a ring clip that you clip on, measure the length from one end of the clip's pincher to the top of the ring or decorative area that covers the ring.

Bottom hems

The hem at the bottom of a window treatment panel not only finishes the treatment, but it also adds weight so the curtains hang well. How big a hem you need depends on the type of fabric you use and its weight. The range is usually 3 to 6 inches. Heavier or thicker fabrics call for a smaller hem. A window treatment panel's hem not only finishes the treatment, but it also adds weight so the curtains hang well.

For sheer curtains, consider adding an extra few inches of hem fabric to add a bit of weight. If you don't like the look of a big hem (one that extends up very far on the curtain or drapery), you can double or even triple the fabric over and tuck it in to create a smaller hem.

If you plan to use a double treatment — hanging one set of draperies behind another set of draperies (for instance, sheers behind opaque fabric draperies) — make the inside treatment's hem a half-inch shorter than the other one, so it doesn't peak out underneath the outside treatment.

Adding length for balloon treatments

Traditionally total balloon length of a valance needs to total one-quarter of your total window length. We don't necessarily agree with that caveat. If you want your valance to be a bit longer for some added protection from the late-day sun, go right ahead! Balloon valance length measurements do need a bit of extra fabric to create fullness and a billowy look. Just add 8 inches to the finished valance measurement to get this fullness.

Balloon shade length measurements need an additional 10 inches to the finished length of your curtain for the appropriate billowy look. For more on balloon-type treatments, see Chapter 14.

Accounting for puddles

To create a puddle effect, pick out a light- to mediumweight fabric. Heavy fabrics don't create a puddle well because they're usually too tough and stiff. To determine the puddle look you want, first use a cotton sheet to test the effect before shopping for your fabric. Some people like a deep puddle with plenty of fabric on the floor, while others just want a ripple or two touching the floor.

To test what you like, puddle a yard of your fabric into shape, and then measure it to see how much extra length you need. Generally, you need to add 6 to 8 inches past the floor to your panel length, but you could add up to a foot if you want a special puddle effect.

Measuring for swags

The key to measuring fabric length for a swag or a swag and cascade is using a flexible tape measure for your swag measurement. Because the swag curves down away from the rod in an arc, you need a measuring device, such as a cloth tape measure, that arcs and curves, too. For more on the swag-and-cascade treatment, check out Chapter 14.

To measure for a swag, follow these easy steps:

1. **Starting from the left-hand side of your window (at the floor, or at whatever spot to which your cascade will hang), measure up to the rod.**

   This is your left-hand cascade measurement.

2. **Next, starting from the top of the pole on the left-hand side, take your flexible measuring tape and re-create the arc of the swag over to the top right-hand side of the pole.**

   This is your swag measurement. You need to measure the lowest part of the draped swag in order to get the appropriate amount of fabric.

3. **Measure your right-hand cascade by measuring from the rod to the end (at the floor, or at whatever spot to which your cascade will hang).**

   This is your right-hand cascade measurement.

4. **Add these three measurements together.**

   Make sure to include a bit of extra fabric to account for any swirling around the rod on either side, plus 1 to 1½ inches on either side for the side hems.

Making and Using Patterns

Some of the projects in this book call for creating patterns. Before you start to make (and use) your patterns, you need to have the right tools. Keep the following tools together in one box or basket, so you always know where they are.

- ✔ Flexible cloth measuring tape
- ✔ L-square (also called a drafting square)
- ✔ Pattern paper or butcher's paper

✔ Scissors/shears

✔ Fabric marker or tailor's chalk (optional)

(See Chapter 5 for specific information about these tools.)

Creating patterns for window treatments

The advantage to making patterns is that you can easily create many panels that will be identical to each other. You can also easily replicate a treatment in many different fabrics as many times as you want, whether for identical windows in the same room, or for future window treatments. Patterns are worth the time and effort if you like to change the look of your windows frequently.

Most patterns for window treatments are big squares or rectangles, for making basic panels, or small rectangles, for creating tabs and tiebacks. However, if your project has any pleats or folds (such as pleated draperies), or parts with curved edges (such as ruffle curtains), you may want to make a pattern for them to keep them consistent and your creation on track.

You can make patterns using plain *butcher's paper* (plain, thin off-white paper that comes on a roll or in a package), or you can buy specially made pattern paper, which has a dot every inch, to help you measure inch by inch and keep lines straight. For more on making a grid with butcher's paper, see Chapter 5.

To begin making your pattern, follow these easy steps:

1. **Lay out your paper on your workspace, and using the left-hand edge as your guide, measure out the pattern dimensions you need.**

   To create perfect corners, use your L-square.

   The little lines of dots that run across pattern paper at the inch markers can help you keep a straight line and to make nice 90-degree angles.

2. **For arched or curved patterns (for example, in the arched valance or ruffle curtains projects), draw your curves freehand.**

   For an arch, start in the center and draw your arch from side to side, or fold your pattern paper in half and cut it to make each side even.

   You're just working with paper. Feel free to mess up and try again, to tape additional paper on if you need it, and even to practice something like cutouts before you begin on fabric. In the end experimenting on paper first can save you time and money.

3. **When you're ready to cut your paper pattern, use a sharp pair of scissors (not your dressmaker's sheers, which are reserved for cutting fabric only) and cut exactly along the drawn line.**

Pattern placement tips

Placing your pattern properly is an important step in making your panel come out right. Keep the following information in mind when laying out your pattern on the fabric:

- ✔ **Pretreating and ironing your fabric before cutting or placing your pattern are vital steps.** If you choose a washable fabric, you need to pretreat it. Furthermore, you need to make sure all the wrinkles and creases are ironed out. If the fabric still has wrinkles, it won't lie flat when you cut it or when you're placing your pattern. (See Chapter 3 for more important pointers about pretreating your fabric.)

- ✔ **Laying the pattern *on-grain* (parallel to the selvage edges) is essential.** Be sure to double-check that your pattern's grain line is parallel with the selvages before you cut your fabric. See the sidebar "Is your fabric on-grain?" in this chapter for more info.

- ✔ **Pinning your pattern in place helps when it's time to cut.** Use a straight pin every 6 inches, making sure that your pin is on the inside of the pattern (rather than on the pattern edge or sticking out of the edge), so that when you're cutting you don't cut down on a pin and ruin your shears.

The following sections offer some additional tips about working with fabrics that have certain textures and prints.

Knowing the parts of your fabric

If you understand the parts of a piece of fabric, you'll be able to place your pattern correctly and cut it properly. The following list dissects a piece of fabric into its important parts that you need to know:

- ✔ **Bias:** An imaginary line that runs 45 degrees between the lengthwise and crosswise grains. To find the bias without a measuring device, fold the fabric diagonally so that the cut end aligns with one selvage.

- ✔ **Crosswise grain:** The grain that runs across the fabric's width. You can always find this edge by seeking out the selvage edges; the width is always perpendicular.

- ✔ **Lengthwise grain:** The grain that runs along the fabric's length. You can always find this grain line by seeking out the selvage edges; the length is always parallel.

- ✔ **Selvages:** The finished edges of the fabric, usually marked with color codes or numbers. The selvages (or selvage edges) always run parallel to the lengthwise grain.

Figure 6-2 can help you identify these parts.

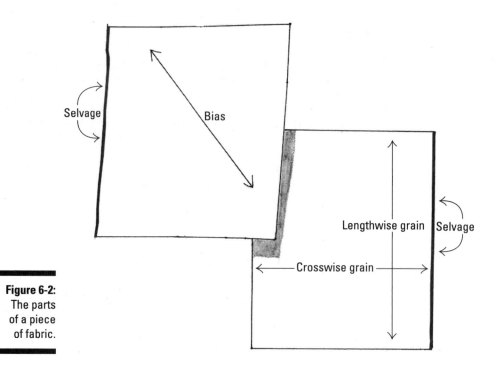

Selvage

Bias

Lengthwise grain   Selvage

Crosswise grain

Figure 6-2:
The parts
of a piece
of fabric.

Working with textures

When you're working with a fabric with a *nap* (a soft or fuzzy, raised texture), such as velvet, velveteen, or corduroy, make sure that all your fabric is facing the correct way when you place your pattern on it. Run your hand along the fabric's length to ensure the nap for each piece of fabric feels smooth from top to bottom. If it's rough or your hand meets resistance, you have the nap the wrong way.

Is your fabric on-grain?

On-grain means that your pattern repeats coincide exactly with the fabric's crosswise grain. Knowing if your fabric is on-grain is important if you want your fabric to hang straight and to avoid a left-or-right-skewing panel that makes you feel dizzy. Verify if the grain runs correctly by placing your fabric on a flat surface and folding back the crosswise edge so that you align the selvages on the sides. Then make a fold to create a crease, and unfold the fabric. Does the crease run into the selvages at exactly the same place in the pattern on both sides? If it does, your fabric is on-grain; if not, save the fabric for a project where you don't have to do any pattern matching.

Working with prints

If your fabric has a small-scale, allover print, you don't have to worry too much about matching the design from panel to panel. They'll "blend" together if your print is petite. However, if you've chosen a print with a one-way design, that is, a print that only looks right going one way, for instance, a red rose with a stem, you also need to make sure that all your panels run the same way, so that the rose is pointing up, not down. The same goes with using horizontal stripes or plaids.

When you're working with medium- or large-scale motifs on printed fabric that need to match from panel to panel, take the pattern repeats into consideration. (For a discussion on decorating with scale in mind, see Chapter 1.) Here's a simple way to match patterns:

1. **Place two widths of fabric so that their right sides touch, aligning the selvages.**

   Fold back the selvage on the top piece of fabric and adjust the fabric so that the patterns are matching.

2. **Using an iron, press back the folded selvage along the fold line.**

3. **Unfold the selvage so it's flat again and pin the two pieces of fabric together along the pressed line, so that the pins cross over the line.**

4. **Gently turn the two attached pieces of fabric over to confirm that the patterns are matching.**

5. **Stitch the seam, removing pins as you go.**

   Don't sew over the pins!

6. **Cut away the selvage edges on both pieces of fabric so that you have a ½-inch seam allowance.**

For medium or large prints, be sure that your pattern repeats are consistent. Place your pattern at the same point on the print each time. For example, if you place the pattern for one panel 1 inch above the top of the red rose, make sure you do the same for each subsequent panels. (For even more information about sewing with prints and patterns, see *Sewing For Dummies,* 2nd Edition, by Jan Saunders Maresh [Wiley].)

Cutting Your Fabric

After you know your measurements, have placed your pattern correctly, and secured it with pins, you can cut the length and width of the fabric to create your window treatment's panels.

When you lay out your fabric on your workspace, make sure you have plenty of room to work and that your shears are in good shape. We don't recommend working on a bed, because the cutting angle isn't good. You want to be at the same level as your fabric so you can cut it straight. If you must work on the bed (or on the floor), consider investing in a good-quality fold-up cutting board, which you can buy at most crafts or fabric stores. It can protect your bed linens and provide a nice, flat surface for cutting.

When you start to cut, place a weight in the center of the pattern and fabric, if you need help keeping your fabric in one place. If you don't have a sewing weight, try a book, or several books.

If you have fabric that ravels, it may benefit from *pinking* (being cut with pinking shears). If so, use your pinking shears after you've cut out your pattern piece or pieces using your regular shears. Pinking shears don't give an accurate line and make your sewing job harder if you cut your pattern with them.

Always cut as close to the pattern's edges without cutting the paper.

Keep these tips in mind, and you'll get great results every time:

- Place your pattern on the right side (that is, the pretty face side) of the fabric.
- Make sure your fabric edges are straight. Align your L-square along the selvage (vertical) edge and with your marking pen, make a line along the perpendicular (horizontal) side. Cut along the line and you have straight edges.

  For solid fabrics, be sure all cuts are made along the exact crosswise grain of the fabric. For printed fabrics that require pattern matching, check to ensure that your fabric is on-grain before you begin.
- Be sure your fabric's nap is going the same way each time you cut a pattern.
- Be sure your printed fabric is going the same way each time you cut and that you've placed your pattern on the same spot each time, following the pattern repeat.
- Pin your fabric in place every few inches, with either straight pins, or safety pins, for more hold (see Chapter 5 for more on pins).
- Cut your fabric evenly and without cutting the paper.

Now your fabric is measured and cut and you're ready to sew! See Chapter 7 or even 14 for some easy projects to get started.

Chapter 7

Making Easy No-Sew and Low-Sew Window Treatments

So you don't sew and don't want to figure out how, eh? That's okay. Who says you have to operate a sewing machine to add a bit of panache to your window frames? Not us. Quick, easy-to-make window treatments are the name of the game when Mark designs rooms on the TLC television program, *While You Were Out.* Just because something packs tons of style doesn't mean it has to be difficult to make.

In this chapter, we show you how to make easy no-sew and low-sew window treatments. What do you require to make all these projects? No need to buy a sewing machine. All you need are a good pair of shears, some great fabric, a needle and thread, a glue gun, some useful accessories, and just a little bit of imagination.

Skip Sewing: What Rings, Pins, and a Little Glue Can Do

One of the best things about window treatments that don't require any, or very little, sewing — we call 'em low-sew draperies and curtains — is you can frequently change them because they're so quick, easy, and inexpensive to make. For example, are you tired of those red velvet swags hanging in your living room? No problem! Pull them down in two minutes and replace them with a pastel-striped valance and a set of sheer curtains. When you've only invested a few hours and a few bucks in window treatments, you won't feel so married to them, and that freedom can liberate your designing impulses.

A few of these projects do require very minimal sewing. In that case, you can sew them by hand. If you're a needlephobe, don't even bother with the needle and thread. Instead you can just glue your project together with a hot glue gun. Clips and clip rings, mini-clip rings, and safety pins (more on this topic in the "Safety pins" section below, and also check out Chapter 5 for more discussion) make quick changes easy, and you don't even have to sew a *rod sleeve* (that little pocket of fabric at the top of a treatment where you push the rod through).

Rings with clips

Rings with clips are an amazingly chic and ultra-easy way to hang curtains, draperies, and valances without all the fuss of sewing. They slip right over a rod and slide back and forth easily, attaching to your fabric with small clips that hang off the rings. These small to medium-size clips resemble the ones that children use to attach their mittens to their coat sleeves. Mini-clip rings are an even smaller version, appropriate for lightweight fabric treatments.

If you decide to use rings with clips, you need to match the strength and size of them to your fabric weight. Metal and wood rings are sturdier than plastic ones. You may also want to check out the tension of the clip and how much fabric you can sandwich in before purchasing. A mini-clip that can handle lace or eyelet may look adorable, but may not be able to handle a heavier-type fabric.

Clips are great to use when hanging curtains, draperies, and valences because they're so adaptable. If you get bored with one style, you only need a few bucks and a little time to change them. Furthermore, cleaning the fabric is a breeze. Separating the clips from the fabric is easy when you're ready to launder or make a seasonal window treatment change.

Make an effort to find curtain clips that complement your decor as well as the curtain or drapery. If your furniture finials or pulls are chrome, try to keep your clips and rings in the silver family. If the treatment fabric you choose is a modern one, look for a clean, unencumbered clip and ring style. (Check out Chapter 20 for great sources for clips.)

Safety pins

If all you want to do is make a rod sleeve at the top of your fabric so you can slide a curtain rod through it, medium to large safety pins are another way to avoid sewing. You only have to measure your fabric evenly across the top width, fold the top of the fabric down, pin it across the "line" where you would normally sew (see Figure 7-1), and slide your rod through. Be sure to attach the safety pins to the back of the treatment so they don't show. (This treatment is perfect for a beach or country house, when hauling a sewing machine up a mountain or over a causeway isn't convenient!)

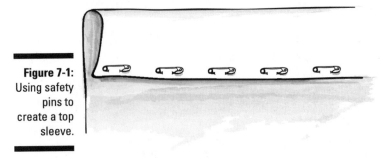

Figure 7-1: Using safety pins to create a top sleeve.

Hot glue

Hot glue from a glue gun is great for adhering fabric to fabric. It sounds cheap and awful — ugh, gunky glue under a cute curtain fabric! — but the fact remains that hot glue and fabric are a match made in heaven. Because fabric is so porous, the glue bonds perfectly, and if you're really careful with your application (not too much, not too little, look out for bumps), and you restrict the use of hot glue to underside areas that people can't see, you can create a great hem or a smooth rod sleeve in a jiffy. And unless you have a particularly nosy significant other, friend, or in-law, nobody will ever know.

Draping Windows: Easy-To-Create Looks

A *swag* is a purely decorative window-top treatment that features flowing or silky-looking fabric. The traditional swag shape is a *scallop* (a curved ornamental edge resembling a rounded shell), but the scarf swag look is a less formal window-top treatment. You can make it from one length of fabric, and it's usually kept in place with a simple decorative rod or special swag holders.

The big challenge with creating swags is getting your drapery right. Don't worry. We guide you through the best way to get the look you love. We also look at fabric considerations, folding and pinning swag fabric, and more. After you get the hang of it, it's easy!

Swagging scarves and throws

Ready-made scarves and throws come in all kinds of wonderful fabrics, from cotton or blended chenille, to wool-blend fabric, to silk charmeuse or silk-synthetic blend fabric. You can use any of them to create an easy window treatment. Scarves are ideal for treatments because they tend to come in silky fabrics that drape well.

But the big bonus in using throws or scarves is they're hemmed, finished, and ready to be fashioned into a simple valance or swag. Here are a few ideas:

✔ You can drape long scarves across a rod at the top of your window to give it a romantic look (take a look at "Creating the swag" later in this chapter for an example).

✔ You can place a series of simple square scarves (see Figure 7-2), either matching or not, across the top of your window to give the look of a valance. You can knot them in place, or use rings with clips to secure them.

✔ You can use throws made of chenille, wool, and other fabric types for a gorgeous and easy way to create a window treatment that keeps the light out. These throws often have fringed edges that look great when hanging from a rod. You can also use a crocheted throw for a crafty or homespun feeling, or any special blanket you want to show off. Just be sure that your rod and brackets are sufficiently sturdy to handle your throw's weight.

With clips and some creative draping and folding, you can create a fantastic and expensive-looking window treatment; check out Figure 7-3. By draping the top edge of the throw over and toward the front and attaching rings at the crease, the two rows of fringe become decorative elements in the curtain.

Figure 7-2:
An easy valance with square scarves.

Figure 7-3:
An easy
drapery
using a
fringed
throw.

Swag baby — with a simple drape

Choosing a swag treatment gives you design freedom with tons of choices. You can make your swag drape symmetrically (with equal fabric on either side or your window) or asymmetrically; have the side fabric extend down a foot, 2 feet, or longer; and you choose how large or small you want your swag "loops and swirls" to be. For a room that needs some privacy, team your swag with coordinating draperies.

Considering fabric

When thinking about making swags, the key word is "silken." Any fabric that makes you think of a soft and silky blouse or dress is what you're looking for, so you can achieve the draping. We recommend a polyester charmeuse for a lightweight swag treatment. Mediumweight polyester crepe fabrics are also a good choice.

As for using prints versus solids, we prefer solids or one-color Jacquards (a type of figured, woven fabric; see Chapter 2 for more about Jacquards), or the simplest, tiniest print. Larger or one-way prints can be hard to use for swags because the fabric drapes across the window in several directions (see Chapter 2 for our discussion on one-way prints). You may want to consider picking a neutral accent color, or a solid color that echoes another color that is already prominent in your decor.

Figuring out your fabric needs

The formula we use to figure the yardage needed for a swag is

- ✔ For the width, allow a two-times measurement of your window, measured from trim to trim. Our window measured 30 inches wide, so our total width was 60 inches.

- ✔ For length (in this project the length is the two areas of the swag that hang down right and left, called the *cascades*), plan to add a measurement that reflects the look you like best. For example, if you want the fabric to hang down so it reaches the midway point of the total length, add half your total window length to each side. Our window measured 60 inches long, so we allowed 30 inches for each cascade. We added 60 inches to our width of 60 inches for a total measurement of 120 inches.

When you have the width and lengths added together convert your inches to yards. To do this, simply divide your total by 36. For example, 120 divided by 36 = 3.3 yards, which you round up to 4 yards of 45-inch wide fabric (you can always use the extra fabric to make a bow or rosette; see Chapter 8 for more).

To figure out how much fabric you need for other fabric widths, see the Yardage Conversion Table in the Cheat Sheet in the front of the book.

Getting your gear together

To get started, you need the following:

- ✔ A few yards of fabric, preferably something that is silky, light- to mediumweight, and that drapes beautifully

- ✔ A decorative curtain rod (the swag wraps around it, so it needs a rod that matches your decor)

- ✔ A box of straight pins (see Chapter 5 for the specifics on straight pins)

- ✔ Needle and thread for hand tacking (or use a sewing machine, if you prefer)

- ✔ A wrist pincushion

- ✔ A piece of tailor's chalk

Draping the swag

The key to getting your swag to look great is to work on the rod:

1. **Drape your fabric over the curtain rod on the actual window you're dressing.**

   Make sure your ladder is secure to prevent falls. You probably didn't plan for an emergency room visit in your window treatment budget.

2. **Carefully pin the folds in place as you go across the curtain, using long straight pins until you get the look you want.**

   Don't be shy — use a ton of pins to keep it secure.

3. **Chalk a light line along the area where your fabric will hang on the rod.**

   After you have your folds in place and you've pinned them, run your chalk parallel with the rod. When you're ready to put your swag on the rod after you've stitched your folds in place, you'll have a clear idea where your fabric needs to go.

4. **When removing the swag fabric from the rod with the pins in place, slide it off carefully.**

   You'll be hand tacking the folds in place (or stitching them with your sewing machine). Don't forget to take out your pins when you're finished sewing.

If you're using a heavier fabric that keeps slipping off your rod as you're pinning, try attaching some double-stick tape to the topside of your rod, which may help keep your fabric in place.

Creating the swag

Follow these easy steps to get great results when making your swag:

1. **Find the center of the fabric, measured perpendicular to the selvage edge, and mark it with straight pins in a straight line (see Figure 7-4).**

   The *selvage* is the finished-looking edge of the fabric where the fabric comes off the loom; you can find the selvage easily because it's always parallel to the lengthwise grain.

Figure 7-4:
Using pins
to mark
the center.

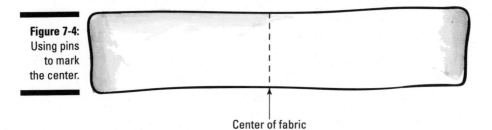

Center of fabric

2. **Toss the ends of your swag fabric over the rod or bar, so that each side has an equal amount of fabric.**

   Your pinned line needs to be in the exact center of the rod (see Figure 7-5).

3. **After you have an equal amount of fabric on either side, make folds where the fabric touches the rod.**

   The folds must mirror each other on each side and the line of pins used for marking the center need to be in a vertical line.

4. **Using your wrist pincushion and straight pins, pin your folds across the rod, being very careful not to pin it to the sheers or other drapery underneath (refer to Figure 7-5).**

   Use plenty of pins and work methodically, pinning the folds to each other to keep the folds in place. You can also add pins where no one can see them, working from the fabric's underside, which can stay in place after sewing. (Be mindful of the pins if you're sewing with a machine.)

5. **While still up on the ladder and after completing all your pinning, take your tailor's chalk and draw a straight line on the fabric parallel with the rod.**

   Doing so gives you a guide for putting the fabric back up on the rod after sewing.

6. **Remove your fabric from the rod and stitch across the folds in the area that will fall behind the rod.**

   Remove your pins as you sew.

7. **Hand tack the folds in the front so that they stay in place (see Figure 7-6).**

   To hand tack your folds, take a needle and a matching color thread and carefully stitch the folds in place by hand.

8. **Slide the rod through the stitched area and use your chalked line to center and arrange the swag fabric to your liking.**

Figure 7-5:
The center
of the fabric
(where
you've
pinned)
needs to be
in the center
of the rod.

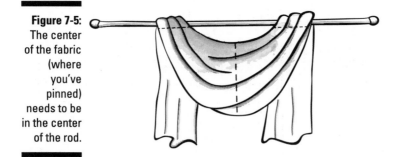

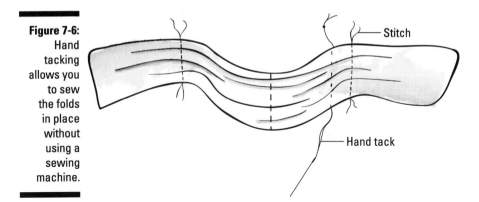

Figure 7-6:
Hand
tacking
allows you
to sew
the folds
in place
without
using a
sewing
machine.

Stitch

Hand tack

Sassy scarf swags

Scarf swags are a wonderful way to dress up a room by adding romance and a bit of softness to already existing draperies, such as sheers. They loop and drape over a decorative rod, jazzing up some plain mini-blinds and providing a touch of elegance to your windows.

The length details of this project are a matter of taste: Some people like long scarves that create a puddle on the floor, while other people prefer a shorter look, perhaps right to the windowsill.

Several pieces of hardware are made especially for holding swag treatments in place (see Chapter 20). But you really don't need to spend a lot of money on these specialty items. To save some dinero, you can use simple knots and a bit of ribbon — and they look just as nice.

Getting started

You need to assemble these items to create your scarf swag:

✔ A few yards of silky fabric

   To determine how much fabric you need for your window, follow these steps using your cloth measuring tape.

   1. **Measure the area of the swag that will go directly over the window top.**

      Start on one end of your rod and measure to the lowest part of the swag, going up and over the rod and back down again until you reach the opposite end of the rod.

2. **Determine the amount of fabric you want to hang down on either side of your window.**

   To do this step, measure from the top corner of your rod to wherever you want your swag to descend.

3. **Add the two amounts of fabric for your total measure.**

   For a standard 30 x 60-inch window, use a swag panel measuring about 180 x 22 inches, hemmed all the way around. The best way to get a piece of fabric with this measurement is to purchase 2½ yards of fabric, cut it in half lengthwise, and then sew the two pieces together end to end (sorry for that bit of sewing work there!). Doing so allows for enough yardage for the loop-around draping effect you want, as well as the two parts of the treatment that wrap and hang down the sides of the window.

✔ Cloth measuring tape

✔ Curtain rod

✔ Scissors

✔ Straight pins

✔ Ribbon (optional)

Making those scarf swags

To create your scarf swags, follow these simple steps:

1. **Find the center of your fabric, measured perpendicular to the selvage edge, and with pins, make a vertical line down the center (refer to Figure 7-4 from the previous project).**

2. **Hang the ends of your fabric over each end of the rod and pin the swirls and folds you like into place (refer to Figure 7-5 from the previous project).**

   Use several pins to keep it secure because the weight of the fabric can undo your work! Don't forget to take the pins out after you have the fabric the way you like it.

3. **Attach your draped scarf swag to the rod.**

   Tying a knot around the bar is the easiest way. Simply wrap your flowing end around the bar and pull it through the loop. Adjust the fabric to your liking, making sure not to tug too hard on the part you've just draped (see Figure 7-7).

   For a bit of extra security, add a small decorative flourish, such as tying and knotting (or creating a bow with) a yard of 1-inch-wide satin ribbon, which wraps around the drapery on the rod (see Figure 7-8).

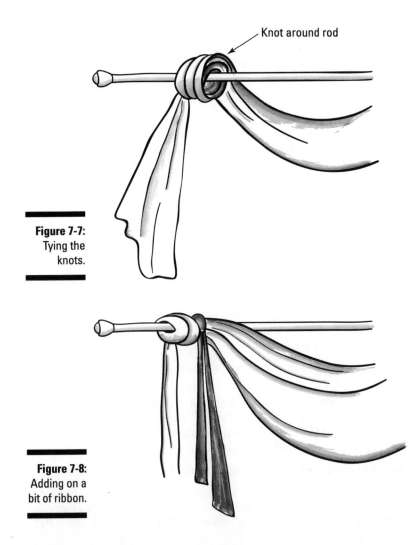

Knot around rod

Figure 7-7:
Tying the
knots.

Figure 7-8:
Adding on a
bit of ribbon.

Hiding Your Unmentionables:
A Simple Lace Shelf Valance

Adding a simple fabric valance over shelving is a great way to hide the
items you use daily but you don't necessarily want displayed. These valances
are just perfect for an open area between kitchen cabinets, to tuck away
everyday nondisplay dishes, or over the sink to hide a shelf of dishwashing
products. Another ideal use is in the bathroom, where a valance can hide

items on top of your medicine chest mirror, adding a bit more discreet storage (check out the color section for an example of this option). Lace also does wonders to soften the look of a hard, tile-lined bathroom, and you can pull in decor colors by choosing a complimentary fabric. (Use a simple 1-inch tension rod for fastest mounting or a flat rod that extends out a few inches from the wall for maximum storage capacity.)

A benefit to using lace: You don't always have to fuss with creating a rod sleeve or finding clips you like. Some laces feature a pattern of small holes, called *beading,* that you can just weave a very thin curtain rod through, or you can snip thin slits through the fabric and insert the rod through them.

Gathering your supplies

Before starting on your valance, make sure you have the following supplies nearby:

✔ One piece of lace, cut to measure

   The key to this project is proper measuring. To determine the correct amount of fabric, use this formula:

   1. **Measure the width of the area you want to cover and multiply by 2.**

      For example, if the area you're working with is 30 inches wide, cut a piece of lace that measures 60 inches wide. (Doubling the width of the window allows the fabric to create natural gathers at the top when the rod is inserted and hung.)

   2. **Measure the height of the area and add 4 inches.**

      For example, if the area height is 18 inches, cut your piece of lace to measure 22 inches long. Because the fabric is two times the width, you'll create natural gathers at the top of the lace when the rod is inserted.

   Although we recommend lace as an ideal fabric for this project, a light, checked gingham is also a good choice. If you decide to use a nonlace fabric that needs a hem, add another inch to each measurement for both the length and the width, and make your hem with the fold-and-fold method. It's just pressing the fabric over so that it tucks under a ½-inch and then sewing a straight line to create a hem (see Chapter 14 for more on this way of hemming).

✔ Cloth measuring tape

✔ Chalk

✔ Iron and ironing board

✔ Sewing machine or needle and thread

Working with lace

Lace adds a feminine and delicate feel to any room. Don't save it only for formal areas; lace is a terrific fabric to add to your kitchen or bathroom.

Polyester machine-made laces are the best choice for simple no-sew curtains because they don't fray and can be cut in many ways. Here are a few other tips:

✔ **Cut your panel width to match the area.** If you want to create side seams, make sure to add an inch on either side.

✔ **For your fabric length, measure down to where you want the treatment to stop and add a few inches to the length.** If you decide to trim your lace along the motif at the bottom, you'll have adequate fabric to do so, plus the needed fabric for creating your rod pocket.

Regarding whether to hem or not, you don't need to hem polyester machine-made lace if you don't want to sew too much; you can cut along the design — say, the rounded part of a heart or the petal of a lace flower — to create a curvy hem. If you're working with handmade lace, don't cut the bottom because it'll unravel, and make sure you create a hem. Cut your lace carefully and sew it either by hand, sew it slowly on your sewing machine using a zigzag stitch, or hem it with a serger.

If you want to make no-sew lace curtains with a lace that unravels or frays, consider using a bit of Fray Check on any areas that have been snipped. Fray Check is like light glue that dries clear and stops fabrics from fraying. (See Chapter 5 for the specifics about Fray Check.)

If you're using cotton lace, always hand wash it before you begin your project to avoid later shrinkage (see Chapter 3 for the best way to pretreat fabric). You don't need to launder polyester lace beforehand.

Making your shelf valance

When creating your shelf valance, follow these easy steps:

1. **Measure 3½ inches of lace at the top and fold it over so that a ½ inch is tucked under (see Figure 7-9).**

2. **With a medium-hot iron, press the lace flat.**

   Be very careful not to burn or melt your synthetic lace because it's prone to dissolve under high heat.

3. **Stitch across at the 3-inch point, with your sewing machine or by hand, to create one large sleeve (see Figure 7-10).**

4. **Create the gathered 1-inch ruffle above the 2-inch rod sleeve below it:**

   • From the fold at the top of your fabric, measure down an inch and draw a straight line across with your chalk.

   • Sew across the line with your sewing machine or by hand (refer to Figure 7-10).

5. Insert your rod into the created rod sleeve, gathering the fabric to create a ruffled effect, and hang your valance.

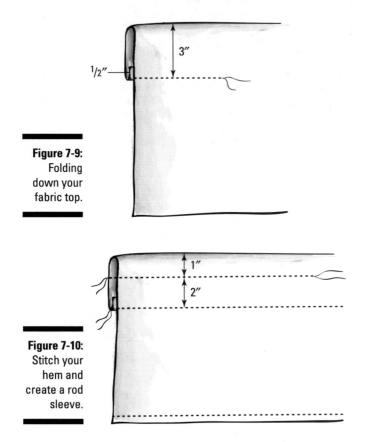

Figure 7-9: Folding down your fabric top.

Figure 7-10: Stitch your hem and create a rod sleeve.

Dollars and cents: A sample budget

To make the simple but sweet-looking lace shelf valance with ruffle top, you only need a few bucks, less than 15, to be exact. Here's how it breaks down:

- 2 yards of polyester lace: $12
- Coordinating thread: $2
- A piece of chalk: 25 cents

Because this project calls for inexpensive polyester lace, you can make a few different colors of this valance and change them at your whim (or for special holidays). What a great way to brighten up that old area over your sink!

Whipping Up Ultrasuede Curtains

These curtains are very simple window treatments that effectively block light and give your room a modern appearance. They're great for young men's rooms, or any room where you want a bit of style without any frills or fuss.

We recommend using Ultrasuede, or if you find Ultrasuede too costly, a less expensive faux-suede similar to Ultrasuede, for these curtains. Ultrasuede may be the most fantastic fabric ever! It never frays, it's washable, and it has the rich appearance of suede without all the hassle. It also comes in many different weights — from lightweight (called "soft" or "light") to heavyweight (called "Ambience"). Mediumweight Ultrasuede is best for the projects in this chapter.

Confusing the right, or face side, and the wrong, or back side, of Ultrasuede is easy to do. Just remember, the right side is the most evenly saturated with color, so use a discerning eye before you begin a project.

Basic Ultrasuede panel

A basic Ultrasuede panel can create an ideal look for any informal room. We suggest you try it in a bedroom, family room, library, or even the kitchen. This panel curtain adds texture with its suede appearance while providing privacy and blocking light and drafts.

Getting your basics together

All you need to complete this project are

- ✔ Any color of mediumweight Ultrasuede fabric

  The measuring is easy. Your panel must be the same size as your window, including the trim mold (for effective sun blocking). If you want a fuller look, add a half-width measurement.

  For example, for a 30 x 60-inch window, use an extra 15 inches, so your width would be 45 inches.

- ✔ Curtain clips
- ✔ Scissors (or pinking shears)

Making the panel

Here's how to make the basic panel, literally 1-2-3:

1. **Measure your window's width and height.**

2. **Cut your panel the exact size of your window.**

   If you want a fuller look, add a half-width measurement.

3. **Attach curtain clips to the top of the panel, about one every 5 inches, and hang.**

If you want to make this project even easier, skip the clips and grab your scissors. Cut small slits at the top of your panel and thread a rod of your choice through the holes. For best results, cut ten 1½-inch vertical slits every 3 inches, starting 1½ inches from the side. These slits need to start about a ½-inch down from the top (see Figure 7-11).

You can embellish your panel however you want, or use pinking sheers instead of scissors to add a different edge. For tips on accessorizing window treatments, see Chapter 8.

You can also cut an inch of fringe for a Western/Native American flair. The panel's length measurement doesn't change if you choose to use these extra flairs.

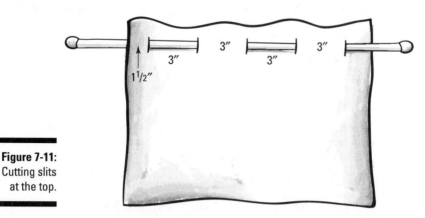

Figure 7-11:
Cutting slits
at the top.

Ultrasuede net curtains

This style of window treatment allows in light and has a cool, organic feel. If you're treating an informal room, such as a den, child's play room, or child's bedroom, that needs a fun focal point, try this project. (Kids especially love it because it allows in light in bits and pieces; they can put their notepads underneath and draw the images the light and shadows create!) This project takes a while to correctly cut, but it's worth the extra effort.

Gathering your supplies

To make Ultrasuede net curtains, you need the following supplies:

✔ Any color of mediumweight Ultrasuede fabric

To figure out how much fabric you need:

1. **Measure across your window for the panel width.**

2. **For the length, measure from the top of the rod to your windowsill and subtract 15 inches to allow for the natural stretch of the fabric when it's hung in place.**

For our project, for an usual 30 x 60-inch window, use a piece of fabric 30 x 45 inches. After you cut the fabric to achieve the net design, it expands and stretches down to cover the 60-inch-long window.

✔ Curtain clips

✔ Marking chalk

✔ A mat knife or X-Acto knife

✔ Safe cutting surface

✔ Shears

✔ Yardstick or ruler

Making your net curtains

To create your net curtains, follow these steps:

1. **Spread your fabric out on your worktable, weighing down the edges if necessary.**

2. **Starting 1½ inches down from the top and from the left-hand side (see Figure 7-12), cut four 6-inch-long horizontal slits, leaving 2 inches in between each one.**

If your fabric panel is narrower, cut off the extra fabric equally from either end. If it's wider, add extra cuts, but always use the cutting measurements we give you for the best results.

3. **Measure down another 1½ inches and starting 4 inches from the left-hand side, cut three 6-inch horizontal slits, each 2 inches apart.**

Continue alternating between the four-cut and three-cut lines until you get to the bottom of the panel.

4. **Attach curtain clips every 5 inches at the top of your panel and hang it from your curtain rod.**

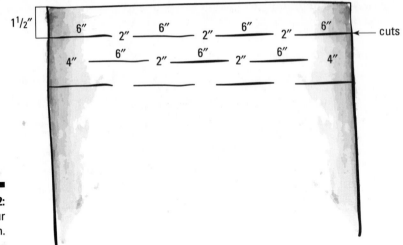

$1^1/_2"$ 6"   2"   6"   2"   6"   2"   6"   ← cuts

4"   6"   2"   6"   2"   6"   4"

Figure 7-12:
Cutting your
net curtain.

Ultrasuede cutout curtains

Another project you can try is one that uses unique cutout designs. The cutouts allow some light through, yet still give privacy. Follow the style we suggest in "Making your strip curtains" later in this chapter, or you can design the cutout motif to suit your decor. Try it in most any room, even more formal rooms like dining and living rooms. You can "fancy" it up by choosing an ornate cutout, or simplify it with an elegant but elemental one.

This curtain is essentially the same as the basic Ultrasuede panel (measure it the same way), but you use an X-Acto blade or cutting knife to create a design similar to a stencil (or you can use an actual stencil if you feel that may help you get the design you want). Try diamonds, hearts, or triangles — simple shapes that are dramatic — or try a scalloped edge on the bottom (see "Creating your cutout curtains" later in this chapter).

The best way to keep your fabric flat and secure when cutting with a sharp blade is to apply a paperweight, heavy books, or other weights on the fabric. (Fabric weights are available commercially, but they're a waste of money.)

Fabric markers and Ultrasuede aren't a great mix: This fabric may absorb the ink a bit too well and not wipe away. If you need to draw your image with something finer than tailor's chalk, work on the wrong, or back side, with a nonbleeding ballpoint pen.

Getting it all together

To start, you need these supplies:

- Any color of mediumweight Ultrasuede fabric

  To determine how much fabric you need:

    1. **Measure across your window to determine your panel's width.**

    2. **For the length, measure from the top of the rod to your windowsill.**

       Your panel needs to be the same size as your window, including the trim mold (for effective sun blocking). If you prefer a fuller look, add a half-width measurement. For example, for a 30 x 60-inch window, use an extra 15 inches, so your width is 45 inches.

- Curtain clips
- Marking chalk
- A mat knife or X-Acto knife
- Safe cutting surface
- Shears
- Yardstick or ruler
- Stencil (optional)

Creating your cutout curtains

To make your cutout curtain creations, follow these easy steps:

1. **Spread your fabric out on your safe cutting surface or worktable, weighing down the edges if necessary.**

2. **With your yardstick or ruler, determine the size of each cutout and the space between each one.**

   You want equal space between each cutout and to the right and left edges of your panel.

3. **Use your chalk to create the pattern you want to cut out of your fabric (see Figure 7-13 for inspiration).**

   Start at the center and work left, and then right, to get an even amount of motifs and spaces across the bottom.

   Consider drawing a light horizontal chalk line across the "top" of your design area. Doing so helps you keep your designs straight when drawing freehand.

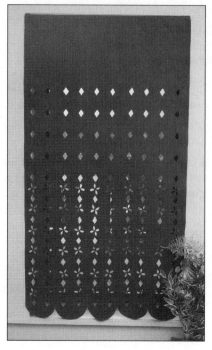

Figure 7-13:
This curtain
features
various
cutout
designs and
a scalloped
bottom
edge.

4. **Cut out your motifs using your knife.**

 Work slowly and take a break from your work once in a while to see if you're doing it right.

5. **Attach curtain clips every 5 inches at the top of your panel and hang it from your curtain rod.**

Ultrasuede strip curtains

This ultramodern "curtain" allows plenty of light to come through, sways in the breeze, and is sure to be a conversation piece among guests. It's created with horizontal panels of Ultrasuede (or other faux-suede fabric) held together with rows of safety pins that add a fun, modern-looking metallic look. Try it in any informal room. You can also try it in doorways, where it allows in sound, air, and light.

For this project, use silver-toned clips if your safety pins are silver, and brass or gold-tone if your safety pins are gold-toned. Buy one large box of safety pins to be sure of the uniformity of the pins. Believe it or not, not all 2-inch safety pins are the same. When they're grouped as in this project, a stray really stands out. You can buy safety pins by the box at dollar stores or at any crafts store (see Chapter 20).

Gathering your supplies

Before you begin, make sure you have these supplies handy:

✔ Any color of mediumweight Ultrasuede fabric

You may want to try alternating colors on different panels — say, blue, red, blue, red — or you can always use the same color throughout.

To determine your fabric needs:

1. **Measure your window width.**

   Your fabric width will be your exact window measurement, including your trim mold (for effective sun blocking).

2. **To determine your length, measure from the top of your rod to the window sill, but plan on allowing for 2 inches of *air space* — the 2-inch area that the safety pins will take up — between each panel.**

   You may need to make your bottom panel a bit longer than the panels above it if your total length isn't an even number. The panel will look fine if you need to take this step. Don't make it shorter; it may seem like your last panel was a poorly planned afterthought.

   As for the proportion of the panels, unless your window is really oversize, stick with the 10- to 14-inch measurement for each panel. You'll get a better effect this way.

   For a 30 x 60-inch window, use four 10 x 30-inch Ultrasuede panels and one 14 x 30-inch Ultrasuede panel, which you can safety pin together. The total panel length with 2-inch safety pin increments is about 62 inches.

✔ Cloth measuring tape

✔ Curtain clips

✔ A measuring tape or yardstick

✔ About 130 two-inch safety pins (all from the same box/boxes)

✔ Shears

Making your strip curtains

To make your strip curtains, follow these steps:

1. **Cut your fabric into the correct panel measurements, as discussed in the previous section.**

2. **Pin the four 10-inch panels together using the safety pins, as in Figure 7-14.**

   The pins need to be an inch apart. Make sure all the safety pins face the same direction and are evenly spaced, to create a professional no-sew look.

Your bottom panel is 14 inches long. Depending on how deeply you pinned your safety pins into the panels, you may need to trim a small amount off to adjust to your window height.

3. **Use your measuring tape or yardstick to ensure an even bottom border.**

4. **Clip your curtain clips onto the top of your curtain and hang with the coordinating rod of your choice.**

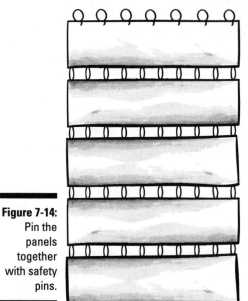

Figure 7-14: Pin the panels together with safety pins.

Fashioning Frayed-Edge Draperies

Frayed-edge draperies are a simple treatment and require no sewing at all, just a few clips for hanging. This treatment lends a natural, organic-looking feeling when the frayed ends move in the breeze. You can use this unique frayed look in any room; try a simple fabric for an informal room, or a more ornate fabric for a formal room.

When choosing a fabric, select one that easily unravels to get the frayed fringe effect. Loosely woven fabrics, such as simple cottons, are great for this project, while cotton twills and polyester fabrics don't work because their weave is too tight. Before you commit to yardage, get a sample and clip a small piece of your loose-weave fabric to test it. Pull threads from both the side and the bottom. Are you getting the effect you desire?

Gather your supplies

Before starting this project, gather these necessary supplies:

- ✔ A few yards of fabric that unravels (see the earlier discussion in the previous section about selecting a fabric that unravels)

  To determine how much fabric you need:

  1. **Add 12 inches to your width measurement.**

     Six inches on either side gives you adequate fabric to allow for the initial trimming and then the fraying process, plus a little fabric to spare in case you want the fringe a bit wider. (Snipping fringe that is too long is a lot less work than taking too much fabric off to begin with and trying to correct it later.)

  2. **Add 7 inches to your length measurement to allow for the fabric that drapes over the top of the treatment.**

  For a 30 x 60-inch drape, use a piece of fabric that is 45 (because fabric doesn't come in 42-inch widths) x 67 inches.

- ✔ Curtain clips
- ✔ Measuring tape or yardstick
- ✔ Shears
- ✔ Sewing machine with appropriate thread (optional)

Get ready to fray

Here's how to fray your fabric and make your draperies:

1. **Cut your panel to the correct measurement.**

2. **To prep your fabric for fraying, trim off an inch or two from the left and right sides.**

   Doing so makes pulling the threads easier in order to create the fringe. (You don't have to trim the top and bottom, which fray well on their own.)

3. **Unravel each side, pulling outside threads one or two at a time.**

   Your goal is to obtain an inch of fringe all the way around, top, bottom, and sides. Keep your measuring tape or yardstick handy so you can keep all your sides even.

4. **When you're done, simply fold 7 inches of fabric over to the front of the panel (see Figure 7-15).**

5. **Add your clips at the top of the fold and hang your panel from your rod (shown in Figure 7-15).**

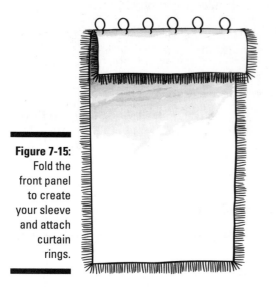

Figure 7-15:
Fold the
front panel
to create
your sleeve
and attach
curtain
rings.

If you don't mind doing a bit of light sewing, consider zigzag stitching around the edges where the fringe starts, as a final step, to secure your frayed fringe. (This step is a nice extra, but the panel still holds well without the added stitching.)

Cruising with Car Wash Curtains

Yep, they look just like the "curtains" you encounter in the drive-through car wash. You get a flowing, festive look with this treatment, which is also terrific in doorways. When the curtain is stationary, you get plenty of sun protection, and when the wind blows through the window, you can enjoy plenty of movement. This window treatment is especially great for kids' rooms, and they're always fun to look at and fun to touch. (Be careful with very young children because they love to tug and pull up on the streamers; it may be a safety hazard.)

You can make these curtains in several different ways. You can use ribbon, Ultrasuede, or plastic shower curtain liners. None requires any sewing and they can all be easily made with just a pair of sharp scissors.

Ribbon car wash curtains

You can use strips of fabric to create this curtain, but we prefer to use lengths of ribbon. One-inch-wide ribbon is a great choice for this project. Don't limit your ribbon color choice to only one shade; try red, white, and blue, all pastels, a variety of colors to create a rainbow-like effect using the full color spectrum, or gradient-toned blues, for a moiré effect, which can give your window a wavy, watery-looking appearance.

If you choose to use ribbons and you're treating an average-size window or larger, definitely look into buying from a ribbon wholesaler to save money (see the resources section of Chapter 20 for more info).

Gathering your supplies

To make this curtain, you need the following items:

✔ Strips of fabric or ribbon

To figure your fabric or ribbon needs:

1. **Take the width of your window and multiply by 2.** That's the number of 1-inch wide ribbons you need.

2. **Take the length of your window, multiply by 2, and then add an inch (which represents the extra length needed to create the knotted loop that holds it in place).**

This measurement represents how long each ribbon needs to be.

For example, for a standard 30 x 60-inch window, use sixty 1 x 121-inch long strips of fabric, or try ribbon cut to the same dimensions, which you knot and hang along the rod of your choice.

✔ Scissors

Making the curtain

Check out Figure 7-16, which is the simplest way to create ribbon car wash curtains, and follow these steps:

1. **Measure your ribbons, allowing for the extra inch of fabric needed to make the loop and knot.**

2. **Cut the ribbons to the appropriate length.**

3. **Loop them around right on the rod of your choice.**

You can do it any way that's pleasing to you. In Figure 7-16, the loop tucks under the downward hanging ends. Just be sure the two ends are of equal length before you pull the ribbon tight to secure your loop.

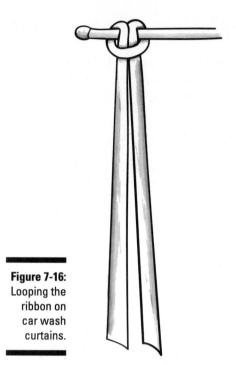

Figure 7-16:
Looping the
ribbon on
car wash
curtains.

Ultrasuede car wash curtains

Using Ultrasuede (or another brand of faux-suede fabric) is another way to
create these fun curtains. You get less of a breezy effect because faux-suedes
are heavier, but you'll get more sun protection, too. Add this treatment to any
informal room.

Getting your supplies together

When making Ultrasuede car wash curtains, use the following supplies:

- ✔ Any color of mediumweight Ultrasuede fabric

    To figure out how much you need:

    1. **Measure your window width and add 15 inches to your measurement.**

    2. **Measure your desired length.**

        For a window measuring 30 x 60 inches, use a piece of fabric that
        measures 45 x 60 inches.

- ✔ Curtain clips

✔ A measuring tape or yardstick, if you have a hard time keeping the strips an even 1-inch wide

You could also use a clear ruler, which allows you to see the fabric better.

✔ Scissors

Assembling the curtain

Follow these simple instructions to assemble the curtain:

1. **Cut your fabric to achieve the correct size panel.**

2. **From the bottom of the panel, cut 1-inch-wide strips all the way up until you reach 3 inches from the top of the panel.**

3. **Attach curtain clips to hang.**

Shower liner car wash curtains

This project is fun, perfect for a child's room. It's an easy way for you to indulge them in their three favorite colors. Check out the discount and dollar stores for shower liners, where they're a bargain, and you can pick up your shower curtain hooks there, too. Red, white, and blue, or red, clear, and blue are nifty combos.

Gathering your gear

To begin this fun project, you need these items:

✔ Three different-colored shower liners (one can be clear)

✔ To get the right measurements for your curtain:

1. **Simply add 15 inches to your window width measurement.**

2. **For length, just snip the shower curtain liner to the length you need.**

For a window measuring 30 x 60-inches long, use a piece of shower curtain liner that measures 45 x 60.

✔ A measuring tape or yardstick, if you have a hard time keeping the strips an even 1-inch wide, or you could use a clear ruler

✔ Scissors

✔ Shower curtain hooks

✔ Clothespins (optional)

Creating the curtain

You can make this curtain in a snap, but don't be afraid to work slowly to get it done right:

1. **Line up the holes of the three shower curtain liners so that you can make sure that your strips line up.**

2. **Clip the three liners together with clothespins if you want to keep the slippery liners from moving as you cut.**

3. **Starting from the bottom, cut each shower liner into a panel that measures 45 x 60 inches.**

4. **From the bottom of each panel, cut 2-inch-wide strips all the way up, until you reach 3 inches from the top of the panel (where the prepunched holes are).**

5. **Hang the layered shower liners on your curtain rod with plastic or metal shower curtain hooks (see Figure 7-17).**

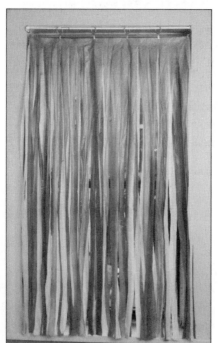

Figure 7-17:
Layered shower curtain liners make a fun and easy window treatment.

Avoiding the Sewing Machine: No-Sew Shades

A nice alternative to curtains and draperies, shades are great for rooms of small proportions, such as half baths, and the two fun shades in this section are perfect for young adult rooms.

Shades with color transfers

Color copy heat transfers are wonderful, and you can make any photo, art image, or original art into a heat transfer at a copy shop. This project is fun for kids, and a nice way to personalize a room.

This project makes one shade, and you can choose any motif: an Andy Warhol–type, four-photo self-portrait; a floral collage; a tribute to favorite music groups past and present; whatever your heart desires. You can make a photomontage of the person who occupies the room, or use this treatment as a tool to designate sides of a room that are shared by more than one child. How about a design of one child's artwork? Maybe you want to try a black-and-white theme: Cut out a bunch of pictures of zebras and go to town. The options are totally fun and truly limitless.

Use a fabric roll-up shade if you can; plastics don't allow the transfer to adhere (but see the note in Step 2 in "Getting started on your shade").

Gathering your gear

When making this shade, you need these basics:

- ✔ Color copy of the image/s of your choice
- ✔ One fabric shade
- ✔ Hammer
- ✔ Mounting hardware to mount shade
- ✔ Sewing machine with zigzag (optional; see Step 2 in the next section)

The art of heat transfers

The best way to do a heat transfer is to place it exactly where it needs to go (check to see if it's straight with an L-square) and iron it on the highest heat your iron has, with no steam. Lift the corner to check your work and see whether it's taking to the fabric. Keep the heat and pressure up. When it starts to take, starting at the top, lift the paper a little at a time until you get to the bottom of the transfer. After you remove the paper, remember to iron only on the back of the shade. You can't directly iron onto the transfer, or it will burn and ruin your iron!

Getting started on your shade

Making this shade is as easy as 1-2-3:

1. **Take your image to the copy shop.**

   The largest color copy transfer the copy shop can make is about 17 x 11 inches.

2. **Follow the directions on adhering a heat transfer the copy shop provides you (if it doesn't, see "The art of heat transfers" sidebar in this chapter).**

   If you can't find a fabric shade, iron your heat transfer onto a white, 100-percent cotton piece of fabric and sew it onto your shade with your sewing machine's zigzag feature.

3. **Put your shade up with your hammer and mounting brackets or other appropriate hardware.**

Clear Contac paper "shades"

You make this "shade" with adjacent squares covered with clear Contac paper, which is a great material to work with for many reasons: It allows in light, while still offering some privacy, and it's cheap and easy to use, so you can change your mind often, or redecorate your window for each season, holiday, whatever your whim.

Sneak a peak at the end of this project to see the finished job (Figure 7-18). This simple project gives any informal room a fun feeling. Consider making this shade for a modern bedroom, where the square panels are echoed elsewhere in your decor. Try it in a child's bathroom or bedroom; it's a great opportunity to let your kids' artwork have a better place to shine than the refrigerator door.

To create a hanging window shade, apply clear Contac paper over equal-size pieces of paper, which laminates the images so they stay in place and the shade pieces maintain their integrity.

Gathering your gear

Before you start, get the following items ready:

- Any kind of interesting paper that matches your decor

  Some ideas include colorful construction paper, a color-page sheet from a newspaper (check out foreign-language newspapers if you're matching an ethnic decor), beautiful wallpaper or wrapping paper, vintage greeting cards, color copies of photos, images from children's books, or anything you like. For kids' rooms, try spelling out names, words, or messages by using a letter on each Contac-covered square.

  To figure out how many squares you need, follow these steps:

  1. **Measure your window length and width.**

  2. **Figure how many identically sized squares you need to reach your windowsill, interspersed with 2-inch clips between each square.**

     Try 4 x 4-inch squares because they break down nicely for a 30 x 60-inch window and provide a variety of images. For a window of this size, use about seven or eight rows of squares, and they'll be ten squares long each, with 2-inch paper clips between each square. You can do the simple math; now get cracking on finding all those images!

- 6 yards of clear Contac paper

- Curtain clips

- Curtain rod

- Hole puncher

- Scissors

- One box of 2-inch paper clips

  Because paper clips can vary in style and color from company to company, use all your paper clips from one box for a uniform appearance.

Making your shade

To create your shade, follow these steps:

1. **Cut your decorative paper into 4 x 4-inch squares, enough to fill your window.**

2. **Apply one layer of the clear Contac over one side of the decorative paper and then the opposite side.**

   Doing so "laminates" the image, suspending it between the Contac paper.

3. **Cut the Contac paper–covered image leaving a ½-inch edge of Contac around each square.**

4. **Punch a hole at the top and bottom of each square, being sure to keep the holes within the ½-inch of clear Contac paper.**

5. **Arrange the squares in columns and attach with large paper clips.**

   Be sure to only punch one hole at the top for the bottom squares.

6. **Attach the top paper clips to your curtain clips.**

7. **String along your rod and hang (see Figure 7-18).**

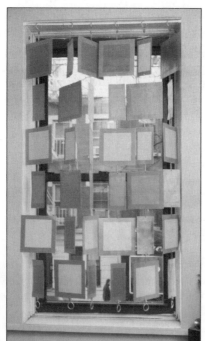

Figure 7-18:
String
'em up.

Chapter 8

Accessorize! Window Details That Dazzle

So you're ready to add even more panache to your window creations, eh? Well, with just a little extra effort, you can customize your window treatments and create fun, one-of-a-kind draperies and curtains that wow your guests.

In this chapter, we show you how to add decorative flourishes to window treatments. We also discuss basic decorations you can add to curtain panels, together with the variety of trims available, the different styles of tiebacks you can use, and how to apply tassels.

Decorating Your Curtain's "Face"

Concerning window treatments, even a bit of embellishment goes a long way. Just like some people apply makeup to their face to improve or highlight their features, you can consider adding a few extra decorative touches in the form of trims to your window treatment's "face," especially if you've chosen a solid fabric. You can also punch up the style of prints by adding even more shine, texture, and dimension to your treatment with paillettes, sequins, rhinestones, studs, and other little extras. Considering how much style these little extras bring and how little time (and money) it takes to add them, you may even want to attach more than one.

Adding fabric embellishments

You can make a wide variety of beautiful extras with fabric and add them to your treatment's face. Just don't forget these few considerations in this section. For instance, use any fabric that pleases you — it can match or contrast with your treatment — but make sure it's a fabric that has enough body (is weighty, strong, or stiff enough) to hold the shape you've chosen.

Rosettes

Rosettes are little fabric embellishments that are associated with the design style of the Regency period (1830s England, when embellishment was robustly, but tastefully applied). They mimic classic floral shapes like roses and *choux* (which resemble cabbage roses). You can use them to accent curves or call attention upward toward valances and swag corners. They're traditionally made from the same fabric as the treatment, but that doesn't mean you can't use a contrasting fabric for your rosettes. Either way, they draw the eye to wherever you place them, so be sure to choose well and to apply them evenly and consistently to your creation.

Consider adding rosettes to our balloon valance project, or to the area where the swag and cascade meet in the swag and cascade treatment, both in Chapter 15. You can also use a rosette to help disguise, if necessary, the area where nondecorative brackets or other purely functional hardware pieces are attached to the wall. You can add smaller rosettes to your tiebacks for added charm (check out "Tweaking the Look with Tiebacks" later in this chapter for more info).

Keep the size of the rosette consistent with the treatment's proportion. If you're adding to a drapery, your rosettes can be larger, but keep them smaller for a shorter curtain.

You can also make easy rosettes from wire-edged ribbon. Start from the center of the flower by curling a bit of the ribbon inward and pinching, so you have a firm center. Then, working outward, move in a circle, pinching to create form and creating the floral shape as you work.

Bows and Maltese crosses

Simple bows comprise two loops and two tails that hang downward. You can create them from ribbon, or use matching or contrasting fabrics. You can add them to the corners of a swag treatment or use them to make pretty tiebacks for any treatment. Bows impart a sweet and homey feeling to curtains, perfect for a kitchen or family room/den treatment.

A *Maltese cross* is also made either from ribbon or fabric, but consists of four loops and no tails, with either a small button or small circle of fabric in the center. It gives a more formal feel to draperies and looks quite elegant in a living room or dining room.

Using paillettes and sequins and Be-Dazzling

Paillettes or sequins can jazz up a window treatment, and rhinestones or studs adhered with a hand-held mechanical applicator (like a Be-Dazzler) are always a universal hit with little (and not so little) girls, so apply them with gusto!

Paillettes and sequins

Paillettes are round, flat, and usually metallic-finished discs with tiny holes at the top, which enable you to attach them to fabric. Paillettes come in two basic sizes — 20 millimeter and 30 millimeter — and have matte or shiny finishes. Some have a mirror-like finish, which especially adds dazzle and shine. Consider adding them to any of the Ultrasuede curtain projects in Chapter 7. We love paillettes on an ultramodern panel treatment as a simple yet dazzling embellishment reminiscent of the 1960s. You can also try adding paillettes to a light drapery or curtain made with sheer or semisheer fabric. When the wind moves your treatment, the paillettes really strut their stuff.

Sequins are similar to paillettes, but they're smaller, their holes are in the middle, and they can come in many different shapes, such as squares, triangles, or circles. You can buy sequins loose or prestrung. The prestrung sequins are lined up and great for applying evenly along seams or hems.

Sequins look great when distributed randomly across a solid fabric, or to mimic a constellation. You can also add them to prints to highlight areas of a motif, such as scattered inside the petals of a flower, or along the "collar" of an animal.

How many paillettes or sequins you add per window treatment is your decision, but keep scale in mind how your embellishments look when viewed from afar. If you're applying paillettes or sequins to a long drapery, don't skimp, or you may lose the effect. On the other hand, if you're applying them to a shorter curtain in a small bathroom, space your paillettes out so the scale is appropriate for the closer quarters.

Adding paillettes does have one major drawback. You have to sew them individually onto the window treatment fabric. If you don't need to use many, you can sew them on by hand. Hand sewing is the easiest way, but you can use a sewing machine, too. Just use a zigzag stitch with the stitch length set to zero.

If you're applying paillettes to a swag treatment, you may want to tape or pin them on — or even hand tack them — while your swag fabric is up on the rod. That way you can see which way the fabric is flowing so the paillettes hang down properly (not stuck in limbo, pointing to the left or right) and give you the look you want.

Be-Dazzling

Applying stones and studs with a hand-held mechanical applicator — the best known and, to our minds, the one that gives the best results, is the Be-Dazzler — is a whimsical and inexpensive way to add a bit of glitz. One by one, you attach tiny rhinestones, studs, or other jewel-like embellishments (with the help of little metal findings that hold them in place) to fabric with the Be-Dazzler, which costs about $20 and is available at many crafts stores. You have plenty to choose from in terms of styles of stones and studs, including

- Artificial pearls
- Clear and colored rhinestones
- Metal mirrors
- Silver- and gold-tone metal studs in star, heart, flower, square, and round shapes

To create a motif or other pattern, consider applying a dot of tailor's chalk to the right side of your fabric to mark where you want to add each stone or stud.

Buy more stones or studs than you think you need. Erring on the side of more is always less frustrating, and a 250-count package only costs between $10 and $15.

After you have your materials picked out, consider the following design ideas:

- Adding rhinestones in a line or swirl on your fabric's face. You also can add these extras to a curtain's trim.
- Scattering stars all across the fabric to create a constellation effect.
- Creating motifs, like hearts, starbursts, or others.
- Spelling out your little girl's name in bright rhinestones.

Your options are limitless. Whatever design you try, you're bound to have fun!

Adding Charm with Decorative Trim

Who doesn't love the notions and accessories section of a fabric store? A coordinating or contrasting trim for your new window treatment adds style and covers up unfinished or not-so-perfectly sewn hems. Use trim to soften the look of a crisp fabric or to draw the eye upward or downward. See Figure 8-1 for a peak at a few of our favorite trims.

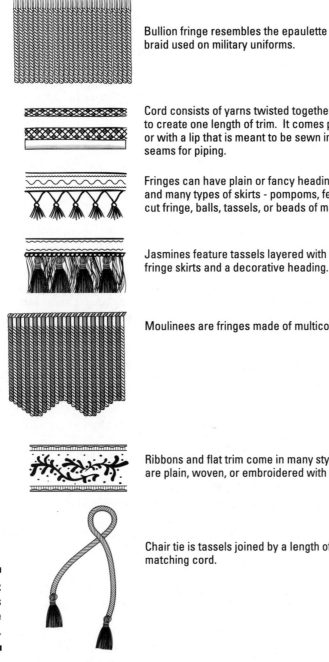

Bullion fringe resembles the epaulette braid used on military uniforms.

Cord consists of yarns twisted together to create one length of trim. It comes plain or with a lip that is meant to be sewn into seams for piping.

Fringes can have plain or fancy headings and many types of skirts - pompoms, feathers, cut fringe, balls, tassels, or beads of many types.

Jasmines feature tassels layered with cut fringe skirts and a decorative heading.

Moulinees are fringes made of multicolored yarns.

Ribbons and flat trim come in many styles. They are plain, woven, or embroidered with motifs.

Chair tie is tassels joined by a length of matching cord.

Figure 8-1:
Various decorative trims.

Budgeting for trim

Though your trim is a smaller part of your treatment compared to your fabric, don't consider it as an afterthought, because trim can be more expensive in total than your treatment fabric. Simple polyester ribbon trim starts out at $4 a yard and goes up, according to fiber content and whether the ribbon was loomed or further adorned with beads or embroidery.

Sometimes you can buy ribbon by the spool (which can contain from 10 to 100 yards, depending on the spool; always inquire about the total length), which can be a better and cheaper way to purchase ribbon. We found polyester grosgrain on a spool for $4.50 for 10 yards and polyester satin for $20 for 100 yards.

Beaded trims are always more expensive. Rayon chenille ball fringe is $4 a yard, while beaded ball fringe is $40 a yard. Tassel fringe starts out at $12 to $14 per yard and goes up. If a trim style is being remaindered, you can get a better deal; look for closeout sales in shops and online.

If you can, buy your trim at the same time that you buy your fabric, simply because mixing and matching is easier when you have the fabric *and* trim selections in front of you. If you must use two sources, keep samples nearby in your color notebook that we recommend and explain in Chapter 2.

Be sure to buy more trim than you think you need. Adding a ½-yard to your measurement doesn't cost much, but it can save time and frustration. Perfectly matching two pieces of trim cut at different times and sewing them together can be difficult to do. It pays in time and frustration to be sure you have enough trim the first time around.

Choosing your decorative trim

Trim needs to enhance the look you're trying to achieve without overwhelming it. Here are some ideas for trims that complement various fabrics and styles:

- ✔ If you want to add a bit of festivity to curtains made from Mexican blankets or from fabric that resembles a serape, try ball fringe.

- ✔ If you have Victorian-style formal velvet draperies, bullion fringe is great (and your cat will love it, too!).

- ✔ If you're going for a Louis XIV look with ornate brocade fabric, add some tassel fringe to complement it.

- ✔ If hanging fringe doesn't suit your taste — you're afraid your toddler will make a day of pulling it off or you want an embellishment with a somewhat less froufrou feeling — consider adding a ribbon trim. It adds a bit of interest but doesn't sway in the breeze (and can't be tugged at by curious little hands).

Rickrack is another great option. This wavy-shaped, lightly textured edging material comes in many sizes and gives an old-fashioned or country feeling. It looks great on informal treatments; gingham cafe curtains with rickrack are a kitchen classic.

✔ If you want to elongate your window's appearance, add trim to the top and bottom of a treatment to draw the eye up and down. You can magnify this effect by choosing a trim with hanging threads, such as fringe or tassels. The longer the trim and the more it hangs down, the stronger the enhancement.

You're not limited to one type of trim. In fact, to add dimension, consider sewing a flat braid trim onto a length of ribbon, and then attaching the adorned ribbon to your curtain or drapery. When the braid and ribbon are the same color or tone, you get a more cohesive textured effect, but a contrasting braid on a neutral ribbon also looks beautiful.

If you plan to wash your window treatment, you have to preshrink your trim. Some trim is washable by hand, but much of it shrinks a great deal when washed — for example, trim with rayon content is especially notorious for shrinking — which pushes your budget up a bit, because you need more than expected.

Test a sample first before you commit to your total yardage. Some trim isn't washable under any circumstances, especially those trims with delicately fringed or tassled skirts or beads of any sort. Sequins that are glued on instead of sewn may pop off when exposed to water. When in doubt, ask a salesperson to evaluate your potential trim purchase, and bring along your project book that contains your fabric swatch and care information from the bolt or cylinder tag.

Attaching fringe trims

Fringe trims usually consist of two parts: the fringe itself (sometimes called the *skirt*) and the top band of fabric from which the fringe hangs (sometimes called the *heading*). This band can be made of braided material, or sometimes it looks like a sheer fabric ribbon.

Needle and thread versus glue

The two ways to attach decorative trim by thread and needle (either by hand or machine) are

✔ Using a topstitch or zigzag stitch and attaching it directly to the fabric

✔ Sewing it into a seam

Most trim has a decorative heading that you can use to topstitch or zigzag stitch into place. However, when the trim features a ¼- or ½-inch heading made of ribbon or a woven lip or edging of any type, it's meant to disappear inside a seam. If you're tucking it inside two pieces of fabric (as between the face of your treatment fabric and its lining), pin or glue stick it between the two seams and sew it together in the same way that you sew in piping (see Chapter 18).

If you prefer, a simpler way of attaching this type of trim is sewing or hot gluing it to the back (or underside) of your treatment fabric, making sure that the ribbon lip is well out of sight.

When the trim is flat and consists of one piece, like ribbon or galloon trim, you need to stitch along the outer edge of one side, and then do the same to the other side. Stitching in the same direction for both sides can help you avoid puckering or pinching.

Another way to attach trim is with glue. Glue from a hot glue gun is a quick, easy way to attach most trims. Some liquid fabric glues are also available on the market that you may want to try; look for one that says, "dries clear and flexible" on the label.

Hot glue and liquid fabric glue are both used the same way: Dot them between the fabric and the trim and press down. Use a weight if you're attaching trim to a heavier fabric. If you're using liquid fabric glue, pin your trim so that it stays in place until the glue dries. Test it out before you make an all-project commitment; use a trim sample and attach it to a fabric sample to make sure you like the quick-and-easy results of glue.

Many people like to use spray adhesive or a glue stick to attach the trim to the fabric before sewing it into place. These adhesives take the place of pins and because they're water soluble, they're only temporary. You need to sew the trim into place after the glue dries.

Tips and tricks

The following are some quick tips and tricks that can make your job working with a trim much easier.

- ✓ **Don't be afraid of corners.** Going around corners to add trim is easy. All the projects in this book call for a ½-inch seam allowance, so simply follow the seam allowance, even around the curves. You may have to fold your trim a bit if the curve is tight; simply take the heading and pin a small pleat in it at the corner and stitch it in place.

- ✓ **Don't stress out your trim!** Never stretch decorative trim to gain length because doing so can cause the area where the trim is attached to pucker or buckle, and otherwise disfigure your project.

If you're trapping the lip or edge of your trim (the nondecorative area) — sewing it between two pieces of fabric into a seam — be sure to check

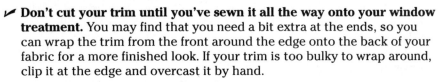

out the instructions for attaching piping in Chapter 18. You need to stitch the trim to the correct side of your fabric, trapping the lip or edge of your trim in the seam allowance (the part that you tuck under and sew to create your finished edge) area of the fabric.

✔ **Don't cut your trim until you've sewn it all the way onto your window treatment.** You may find that you need a bit extra at the ends, so you can wrap the trim from the front around the edge onto the back of your fabric for a more finished look. If your trim is too bulky to wrap around, clip it at the edge and overcast it by hand.

✔ **Don't remove the chainstitch on trim with ornate fringed skirts.** The stitching keeps the skirt yarns flat. Don't remove it until you're finished attaching it, because the stitching keeps the fringe out of the seam when you sew, and it also keeps it from getting unruly around hot or even regular glue.

Adding weight with beaded fringe

Beaded fringe is a type of trim that features tiny rows of beads that hang vertically, usually from a length of decorative braid, but sometimes from a length of sheer ribbon. Some absolutely stunning beaded fringe styles are available, including glass beads, wooden beads, plastic beads, and bead alternatives such as shells and buttons.

Besides adding charm, beaded fringe also has a utilitarian advantage: It adds weight to curtains and draperies, so they hang better. Glass bead trims obviously weigh more than plastic and wood, so keep that in mind. You want to match your beaded trim weight to your fabric weight as closely as possible. If you're using a sheer fabric, be sure that it can support the weight of real glass without ruining your treatment's drape. If not, you may want to go with a glass substitute. Try plastic (usually made of acrylic, which can also be a real money saver), or even a light wood fringe. Heavier draperies or curtains can always support glass-and-braid trims (for more weight, add special curtain weights; see Chapter 4). You can pin your trim on fabric before you sew to test it.

You can attach a beaded trim with a decorative heading by hot gluing it or sewing it by hand or with a machine. If you decide to use a sewing machine, work very slowly. Machine sew both edges of the braid to keep it firmly in place, protecting the beads from damage as you go; you can cover them with masking tape. The braided heading usually has two lines of stitched thread in place, employed in its construction. You can sew over these stitched lines as a guide and to prevent an overabundance of thread on the heading's face. Tuck the beaded trim attached to a length of nondecorative sheer ribbon into a seam so that no one can see the ribbon. Sew it with a zigzag stitch, as in Figure 8-2.

Figure 8-2:
Sew the
fringe onto
the fabric,
watching
out for the
beads.

Edging curtains with ribbons

Adding ribbon to the bottoms and along the edges of curtains is a nice way to incorporate a bit of color, texture, or pattern to solid curtains or more drama to printed ones. First, pin or use a glue stick to set your ribbon in place and then attach it using a zigzag stitch on each edge of your ribbon, as in Figure 8-3, sewing all the way across both edges.

If highlighting the zigzag stitch complements your treatment's overall look (say, for a crafty or ethnic design; see Chapter 10), consider using a contrasting-color thread.

You want to find ribbon that has a bit of heft or texture or both, to complement the heavier weight of decorator fabrics. Try grosgrain ribbons or any patterned or textured ribbon. Very thin satin or sheer ribbon is pretty and works well on a sheer treatment, but it's slippery, sometimes hard to sew and handle, and tends to snag and show dirt. If you sew well, try it out. Otherwise, you may want to save it for wrapping birthday presents and creating hairstyles instead.

Figure 8-3:
Set your
ribbon in
place and
then zigzag
stitch it
to your
treatment.

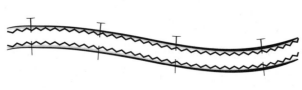

Tweaking the Look with Tiebacks

Tiebacks are material that you wind around your drapery or curtain and then loop over a hook attached to the wall, providing just the right finishing touch.

They're fun window treatment accessories that provide you with another chance to show off your creative side as well as allow light into your room. Depending on where you place your tiebacks, your curtains adopt a different shape and silhouette, and let in differing amounts of light. For example, placing your tiebacks high (more than halfway above the middle of your treatment length) allows in more light; placing them low allows in less. Take a look at Chapter 4 for an illustration of different tieback placements.

If you chose a fairly neutral or one-color fabric for your window treatment, but still want to add a bit of flavor to your creation, a tieback can be a great way of picking up a contrasting color or motif from elsewhere in your decor.

Of course, because tiebacks have a functional aspect, they have to work, not just look great. When you consider how to make your tieback, keep in mind the weight of your drapery or curtain. A lightweight treatment can employ a tieback made from nearly any material, and a light cup hook is enough to keep it in place. However if you're using an ornate or heavyweight fabric for your treatment, you need to use a fabric of equal weight, and you may need to use a *molly bolt* (a securing device that expands inside the wall) to attach a substantial hook to your walls for a tieback strong enough for your curtains.

Creating basic fabric tiebacks

Fabric tiebacks are just long rectangles of fabric with plastic hooks attached at their ends, or that are tied or knotted together at each end to create a loop. Grab your cloth measuring tape; you need it to make these easy tiebacks. To make yours in any fabric that pleases you, follow these steps:

1. **Hang your drapery or curtain and scoop the fabric away from the window toward the frame.**

2. **Loop your measuring tape around the drapery or curtain so it mimics a real tieback and note how many inches of tape you need.**

   If you plan to create a tieback that ties into a knot or bow, be sure to add a few extra inches for adequate fabric to create the decorative ends.

3. **Add 1 inch for a seam and you have your length.**

   For your width, consider the weight of your window treatment fabric and the look you want to achieve. Will your tieback fabric be contrasting, and so may be better shown off with a wide tieback? Perhaps a 5-inch tieback would work. Do you want your tieback to "disappear" into your treatment, and so a thinner tieback may suffice? Perhaps a 2-inch tieback is the ticket. Whatever width you decide to use, double the width and add 1 inch for your seam allowance. For example, if you want a 2-inch-wide band, your width measurement needs to be 4 inches plus 1 inch for the seam allowance for a total of 5 inches.

4. **Lay out your fabric and cut your fabric.**

5. **Using a ½-inch seam allowance, sew your fabric in a long tube with the wrong side facing out.**

   Sew one end of the tieback.

6. **Using a ruler, chopstick, or letter opener, push the fabric inside out so the right side is showing.**

7. **Tuck a ½ inch of fabric on the open end in and hand tack it closed, or use hot glue to seal the end.**

8. **Hand sew on two plastic or wood rings at the ends, or create your knot or bow at the end.**

9. **Repeat for the second tieback and you're done!**

Traditional tiebacks

Just like window treatments, tiebacks can be traditional or a little funky. If you have a traditional-looking window treatment, you may want to consider these traditional tieback styles:

- ✔ **Lined, shaped tiebacks:** Used in more formal rooms, these tiebacks are created with a pattern and feature a variety of shapes, such as crescents, scallops, or round-edged rectangles. The tieback is often lined with coarse, glue-stiffened buckram backing to keep its unusual shape.

- ✔ **Plaited tiebacks:** *Plaiting* is a way of braiding fabric or trim together so they become as one. You can make this style by plaiting three pieces of material together and sewing the ends. You can also make them with ribbon, cord, or any other type of trim that pleases your eye.

- ✔ **Ruffled tieback:** Attached to a ½- or 1-inch strip of fabric, this type of tieback often complements a ruffled window treatment.

Don't forget about holdbacks

Holdbacks are the "hard" version of tiebacks; they're usually made of iron, aluminum, and other metals. Decorative hardware tiebacks can be a durable and stylish alternative to fabric, especially when you have quite a lot of fabric, or a particularly heavy fabric, to hold back. Some look like large, decorative hooks and are called loop style, while other styles may have *projection arms* that stick out from the wall with some sort of motif at the end (a fleur-de-lis, a star, a flower) where the fabric settles into place — these are called knob-style holdbacks. (Check out Chapter 4 for more info on hardware.)

You don't have to use fabric for your tiebacks, even for traditional ones. Consider these other materials:

- ✔ **Chair tie:** We really like using chair tie for creating tiebacks. Chair tie (sometimes called chair tie tassel) is a trim that usually comes in 20- or 30-inch lengths and consists of decorative cord that features 3- or 4-inch-long tassels at both ends.

- ✔ **Matte colored cord:** Cord is an easy way to create tiebacks. Decorative cord comes in many colors and sizes, from ⅛-inch to an inch in diameter. Go for the thickest cord you can find when your curtains or draperies are made from heavier fabric.

- ✔ **Rayon cord:** Rayon cord tends to have a fancy, shiny finish that looks great as a tieback for treatments made from silks, sateens, or any type of shiny-finished fabrics.

- ✔ **Rope:** Consider making tiebacks from different varieties of rope to add a more masculine feel. Crafts stores stock white rope, raffia, jute, sisal, and other types of fibers.

We like it when the tieback materials match or complement the curtain rod's style, although they too can stand alone as distinctive design elements (see Chapter 3).

Alternative tiebacks

Tiebacks need to function, and they need to look good doing so. That said, you don't always have to use store-bought fabric to do the job. Look around your house. You may already have the material hanging around that you can use, or you can visit a secondhand store, local thrift shop, or hardware store with your eyes peeled for anything funky yet functional.

Although some may sound a little whimsical or kooky, consider this list of alternative tiebacks that may just inspire a related idea:

- ✔ A necktie is the perfect length for making a tieback. Stitch two or even three together for a wider tieback, or use a single one for a narrow style. Pick them up cheap at a thrift store, garage sale, or flea market, or raid a male relative's closet.

- ✔ Colored ribbons work well. Just braid three different colored ribbons together to create a simple rainbow-effect tieback.

- ✔ Rope is terrific for adding texture to a jungle- or organic-themed room. Are you thinking of using a tropical print fabric for a window treatment (perhaps for a child's room or a bathroom)? Consider braiding three pieces of rope together to make a sturdy tieback, one worthy of Tarzan.

You can use one or more tones or colors, but be sure to secure the ends by sewing or hot gluing them all together.

✔ Premade fabric rosettes are feminine additions to any style. Pin, stitch, or glue fabric rosettes from the crafts store in a line, from one end to the other of your tiebacks. (Check out the "Rosettes" section earlier in this chapter.)

✔ Fishnet can work wonders to complement your rooms with nautical or fishing themes. You can buy fishnet fabric or cut up a pair of light-colored fishnet stockings (look for the cheap ones made mostly of cotton, with no or not too much stretch), and dye the material to complement a dominant color in the curtain fabric.

✔ Bandannas or vintage lace handkerchiefs are perfect for rooms with vintage styles.

✔ Inexpensive beaded necklaces or Mardi Gras beads make fun, festive tiebacks, making for a really glamorous look for a boudoir window treatment (if you're lucky enough to have one!). Small metal findings at the ends of necklaces make attaching your tiebacks to cup or other hooks especially easy, too.

Similarly, choose an ethnic-themed necklace to complement an ethnic design. Try jade or faux-jade for a Far East look, African bead work to complement mud or kente cloth, and so on. If you can't find two necklaces that match, buy beads and string your own using fishing line.

✔ Tinsel, garland, tiny metallic Christmas tree ball ornaments, or artificial mistletoe sewn or glued to artificial vine from the crafts store all are perfect for the holidays. Similarly, wire-edged ribbon — the kind of ribbon you use to make big bows on holiday presents — makes great tieback material. Just wrap the ribbon around your fabric and twist the ends together, securing them behind the drapery fabric with a hook or nail. Seek the widest and strongest ribbon you can find to ensure that your tiebacks hold well.

✔ Seashells (look for the ones that wash ashore with the hole already in them), acorns, sea glass, dried flowers, gumball machine charms, anything that strikes your fancy, look great sewn onto any plain tieback.

✔ Crocheted yarn (or other materials, even fabric strips) can match any dominant color in your fabric.

✔ Vinyl or faux leather belts offer an ultramodern style. Just snip a belt, tuck the ends under for a finished look, and then seal using hot glue. Attach little plastic hook eyes, or rings, to the belt ends with heavy-duty thread, so you can attach them to the wall with cup hooks.

✔ Interwoven artificial flowers from a crafts store can match a floral motif or spice up a plain-colored fabric treatment. As long as you stay in the same color and flower families, you can't go wrong. This look is a really adorable for a little girl's room.

From telephone to tieback

One of the cutest window treatments we ever saw was a pair of curtains that hung in a small city-apartment kitchen. They were made from fabric that featured an all-over pattern of red, white, and pink telephones, and the tiebacks were constructed from the cord from an old 1960s-style pink princess telephone. The two curly-cues at the end were snipped and sealed with glue to create loops that provided a ring from which to hang the tiebacks (from simple cup hooks).

Tassels: The Final Touch

Tassels consist of ornately looped and tied thread, yarn, or string, and they add a festive, decorative touch to fabric creations.

Larger tassels look great hanging at the tops of your window treatments and they're also nice to add to your tiebacks, which we talk about in the "Tweaking the Look with Tiebacks" section earlier in this chapter. You can buy tassels in many colors and sizes at your fabric store, but you may also want to consider making your own. It's really easy!

If you want to make your own, start by choosing your tassel string, which needs to be a thicker thread like embroidery thread or any yarn. (Don't use sewing thread because it's too thin.) You can use different yarns or threads for different looks. You can choose from fluffy or nubby (for a crafty look), shiny or silky (to match a more formal fabric, such as taffeta, damask, doupioni silk, or sateen), or smooth and matte (nice to complement a faux-suede microfiber fabric like Ultrasuede). One spool of thread or skein of yarn is plenty to make one tassel, and you may even be able to make two, depending on the size of the tassel you need.

Gathering your supplies

To start creating your tassels, get these supplies:

- 1 piece of cardboard, cut to size

  For this project, we chose a piece of cardboard 6 x 2 inches to create a tassel 6 inches long.

- 1 spool or skein of decorative yarn or thread (enough for one to three tassels)

- Scissors

Making your tassels

To create your tassels, just follow these steps:

1. **Wrap your yarn or thread around the longer side of the cardboard about a hundred times (yes, we said 100 times).**

   You're wrapping the thread into a 6-inch-long loop.

2. **Cut a piece of yarn or thread about 10 inches long and slip it through the loop formed by the wrapped yarn/thread at the top of your cardboard and then tie it in a tight knot (see Figure 8-4).**

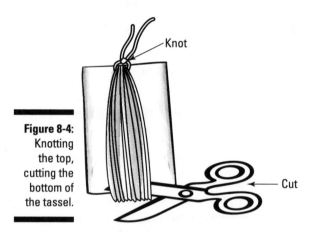

Knot

Cut

Figure 8-4:
Knotting
the top,
cutting the
bottom of
the tassel.

3. **Cut the bottom of the tassel evenly along the bottom of the cardboard (see Figure 8-4).**

4. **Cut a piece of yarn/thread that measures 3 feet (36 inches) long to wrap tightly around the neck of the loop you tied and cut in Steps 2 and 3 as many times as it will go around.**

   Leave enough yarn/thread on the ends so you can tie them in another knot (see Figure 8-5).

   Hide the leftover ends of your yarn/thread in the fringe of the tassel and make a loop at the top so you can hang your tassel.

5. **Trim the bottom of the tassel so that the strands are even.**

   You're done! Now add the tassel to the curtain at a top corner by threading the loop through your rod, or you can attach it to a curtain ring. You can add it to the middle of your curtain to highlight your tieback by threading the tieback through the tassel loop, and then situating the tassel where you like.

Figure 8-5:
Wrapping
the loop to
create the
tassel top.

You can adjust your tassel's size by shortening or lengthening the cardboard. The larger you go, the thicker the string or yarn you'll want to try. Experiment with thread or yarn that you already have at home.

Chapter 9

Quick Fixes and Timesaving Techniques for Window Treatments

. . . .

In This Chapter

▶ Fixing (or covering) your mistakes

▶ Taking shortcuts and making the best use of your time

. . . .

So what happens when your exact measurements are a bit off or you accidentally cut a hole in your window treatment fabric, but you don't want to or can't afford to start over? No problem.

This chapter offers you a few ways to save the day. From too long to too short, from crooked curtains to imperfections, we help you fix whatever problem your window treatment may have. You may even make your creation look better! In addition to quick fixes, we also offer a few timesaving tips to keep you right on track.

No Fretting Over Those Inevitable Mistakes

Even the most talented people who sew make mistakes. Before you throw your fabric in the trash or have a neighborhood bonfire, try these few suggestions to help fix whatever ails your creation.

Lengthening too-short curtains or draperies

Did you measure your fabric twice, cut it, sew the hems, and then while hanging your new curtains realize that they were too short for your window? Breathe deeply. Don't tear them down in disgust. We have the perfect solution for you.

Adding a contrasting fabric at the bottom of too-short curtains is a simple way to get the length you want. It's also an opportunity to give more panache to your curtain or drapery. You can also consider sewing a print to the bottom of a solid curtain for a bit of added style. For example, red-and-white checked gingham sewn to a solid white, red, blue, or even yellow kitchen curtain is attractive. You can also add a piece of wide eyelet lace to a curtain bottom to get adequate length. To give your treatment a cohesive feel, consider using a bit of the added fabric to create your tiebacks, too.

When adding fabric to the bottom of your treatment, follow these steps:

1. **Remove the sewn hem using your seam ripper.**

2. **Measure to find the length of fabric that you need to add, allowing for a ½-inch seam allowance on the existing treatment.**

3. **Add a ½-inch seam allowance and at least another 2 inches for a new hem to the new fabric length to be added.**

4. **Cut out and then attach the new fabric at the bottom of your too-short curtain or drapery using a straight stitch and a ½-inch seam allowance.**

5. **Press your fabric, rehang it on your rod, and pin your new hem (this time you'll get it just right!).**

6. **Take the treatment down and stitch your hem.**

If you're adding a narrow trim or lace for just a bit of extra length, take your hem out with a seam ripper, press it flat, and add the trim or lace with a zigzag stitch to the bottom edge.

Shortening too-long curtains or draperies

If you don't want to take your curtains down and re-hem them, consider draping your curtains through holdbacks or tiebacks in a different way to shorten the total length:

1. **Attach your tiebacks somewhat higher than the center of your window and a bit farther to the left and right than the outside frame.**

2. **Loop the fabric through the tiebacks, and then balloon the fabric over the tiebacks, pulling the fabric down and toward the center of your window.**

   The larger "poof" from the balloon effect picks up some fabric slack.

Check out the illustrations in Chapter 4 to get some other ideas for achieving a fuller look with tiebacks.

Balancing uneven curtains or draperies

When hanging your curtains, you notice that one panel is longer than the other. What do you do? You can take them down and resew them, of course.

If you don't want to do all that extra work, consider something else. If your treatment has a rod sleeve, you can use a tension rod to save the day. Thread the tension rod through the rod sleeve and see if you can position the tension rod so that the panel is even. Your tension rod will be slanted higher on one side than the other and will look a bit funny, so you may want to whip up an easy swag or valance to cover up the top of the treatment (see Chapters 7 and 14 to find out how to make swags and valances in a jiffy). That added top part makes your window look even better. Wow, you've made something gorgeous out of your mistake!

Using accessories to cover holes, rips, or stains

Yikes, where did that hole come from? Instead of blaming yourself, take this opportunity to add a bit of fun to your window with an added design detail, such as appliqués, buttons, and bows. These problem solvers also work well when you're dealing with slightly damaged fabric you picked up inexpensively, and which you knew you'd need to finesse to get a great-looking treatment (see Chapter 2 for more on deciding when it's right to pick up flawed fabric).

When crafting your cover-up detail, make sure it looks like an intentional part of the treatment and that you apply it creatively, proportionately, and equally. The following points are also important to remember when covering holes, rips, or stains:

> ✔ Be sure that the size of the detail matches the treatment's proportion.
>
> ✔ Be sure to add the detail to each panel in generally the same area, even those without any stains or holes, so the entire treatment maintains a cohesive, balanced feel.
>
> ✔ Have fun deciding where to place your details. You could create lines, zigzags, heart shapes, swirls, or any pattern that pleases you.

Always choose your design detail to match your decor and the "feel" of the window treatment. For example, is the window treatment for a child's room, play room/den, or other informal room? Keep your design detail simple: bows made from simple ribbon, buttons shaped like animals or in bright colors, and the simplest appliqués. Is the treatment for a formal area, such as a dining room, living room, or master bedroom? Use an ornate or embroidered ribbon to create bows, or choose one-of-a-kind buttons or a line of beautiful sequins to cover a rip or hole (check out Chapter 8 for more ideas).

Appliqués

Appliqués are decorative embellishments that you sew or glue in place. They, can help cover a hole, rip, or stain in a window treatment, and appliqués are easy to attach. Simply pin them in place or use a glue stick. Pick a thread that matches the appliqué's background and use a straight stitch all around the border to sew it in place. You can use your machine or you can hand sew them on.

You can buy appliqués at a fabric or crafts store or make them yourself. Cut them out of nonraveling fabric like faux-suede or felt, or use a serger to finish the edges of a homemade appliqué made from another type of fabric (see Chapter 5 for more information on sergers).

If you've used a delicate fabric, such as silk or a sheer fabric like voile or batiste, for your treatment and there's a chance the rip, cut, or hole might rip and extend farther out from underneath your appliqué, first mend the fabric with a zigzag stitch before attaching your appliqué. The stitching doesn't have to look great, it just has to give your treatment a chance to "heal" under the appliqué.

Buttons

Buttons are a great way to add weight to a curtain and add a fun, whimsical feel. Sewing on buttons does take a bit of time but the effect is worthwhile. Look for flat buttons that lie flush against the fabric; they can conceal flaws better because they completely cover the flaws. Be sure to mend the fabric underneath so that you have a smooth surface over which to sew the button. Then add your button over the flaw, making sure to add some additional buttons elsewhere on the treatment so it looks like a design detail.

A complimentary row of buttons along the bottom of your curtain or drapery looks terrific and gives a homey, crafty look. For a child's room or kitchen, try a polka-dot pattern in a wide variety of sizes; it's a great way for young children to learn their colors and sizes.

To attach a button by hand, first mark the spot where you want it with a piece of chalk or fabric marker. If you're attaching a row of buttons, use a ruler to space them evenly and to keep your row straight. Choose thread that closely matches the button's color, not the fabric underneath, and thread your needle.

If you're sewing a button that goes through a buttonhole, sew it with some slack. If you're sewing a decorative button, sew it as tightly to the fabric's face as possible. Go through the holes a few times and knot the thread on the back of the panel so the threads don't show.

Bows

Bows made of ribbon are another way to cover holes or flaws. Choose wire-edged ribbon to create bows with specially shaped loops. You can also create bows from strips of fabric. Consider adding small Maltese crosses and rosettes, as well (see Chapter 8 for more on these embellishments).

Paillettes

Paillettes, which are round, flat, and usually metallic-finished discs with tiny holes at the top are another quick cover-up. (You can read all about them in Chapter 8.) Because quite a few large, shiny paillettes go a long way stylewise, you can get away with adding fewer, and you can save a buck or two.

Weighting curtains that just won't hang well

Sometimes the reason a curtain doesn't hang well is its fabric is just too light to acquire a shape. You can add weight to your curtains in a number of ways, such as the following.

✔ You can sew heavy buttons to the bottom as a decorative touch.

✔ You can add a few curtain weights, which are available at crafts and fabric stores. They're tiny metal pellets wrapped in fabric that you sew to the bottom.

If you want to save a little money, don't buy the curtain weights. Just open up a few stitches on your bottom hem, hot glue some pennies or nickels inside the bottom hem of your curtain, and resew the hem.

How to cover a multitude of sins

Okay, so you messed up. Crooked stitching, a hole or two. Hey, it happens. Who says you can't turn the tables and use your mistake as a design detail? Mistakes that are well covered are no longer mistakes at all. (Moms with young children, these tips work equally well to cover up stains that don't "magically disappear" like on the TV detergent commercials.)

Here are a few great combinations to consider:

✔ Cafe, crisscross, or casement curtains look lovely with fabric bows sprinkled around. Use thin ribbon to make your bows and stitch them in place all over your fabric's face.

✔ Add some cut-felt fish, sharks, jellyfish, anchors, boats, and sea plants to your kid's room curtains to cover up holes (or stains) and add a bit of the ocean to the room. Other great themes include the ABCs, dogs and cats, and barnyard animals. Grab your pinking shears to create "fur" on fabric creatures (see Chapter 5 for more on pinking shears). And button eyes are always a classic look. Create multisize polka dots, different balls from various sports, or trucks and cars (stencil kits are available at crafts and fabric stores if you're not artistically inclined).

✔ Add a few sequins to a simple leaf- or flower-shaped appliqué for something truly elegant.

✔ Use a decorative trim, like rickrack, to create "stripes," either vertically or horizontally, across the face of a treatment panel. Arrange your stripes to cover a flaw in your fabric's grain or to cover the damage done by a pair of wayward scissors. If your sewing machine got a bit out of control and your seams are a bit wavy, you can use rickrack to cover them up, too.

✔ Patch squares of contrasting denim fabric randomly on your panels to give a rustic, country feel. You don't have to finish the edges because the frayed effect adds to the look.

✔ Press on patches. Is your curtain stained, but you just can't bring yourself to do any more sewing? Also available for all you no-sew fans is iron-on fabric meant to be used as knee and elbow patches for clothing. You can cut it into different shapes and easily press it on with an iron.

✔ Use glitter glue. Another alternative is to pick up some glitter glue and use it to create a motif that fully covers the stain. Use a marker to draw the border of the motif around the stain, and then use it as a guide to fill the area in with glitter glue. It dries smooth and shiny; kids just love this stuff.

Uniting panels that don't "meet"

Sometimes, despite your greatest effort, the medium- or large-scale repeat patterns don't meet when you mount your treatment and draw the two panels together. If this bothers you, you can try adding a solid fabric in a contrasting color to the center edges. Doing so adds another attractive design detail to your room.

You can also add solid fabric in a contrasting color to your panels' center edges if you didn't properly estimate the fabric fullness for the look you want. Doing so creates a bit more width to your panels.

See the steps in "Lengthening too-short curtains or draperies" earlier in this chapter to add fabric to the sides of your panels; it's the same concept.

Taking Shortcuts That Nobody Notices

We believe that shortcuts don't have to lead to shoddy or sloppy work. In fact, you can make your life easier and still get an attractive end result. This section includes a few ways to speed up your project-making time and maybe even save a bit of frustration in the process.

Using trim to hide selvages

The *selvages* are the edges where the fabric comes off the looms, and they're usually cut away and discarded because they sometimes have writing on them or they don't conform to the look of the rest of the fabric. If you plan to cover over them, this isn't an issue so you don't have to cut them away at all. Covering over the selvage with trim is a great way to get a bit more width from your fabric.

Keep in mind that each piece of fabric has a different size selvage. Make sure the trim you choose is wide enough to cover the entire selvage.

You can attach your trim with hot glue, iron-on bonding tape like Stitch Witchery, or another adhesive product designed for fabric use. To sew it in place, stitch it securely onto your fabric along both edges using a thread color that matches the trim. When using a sewing machine to attach trim, work slowly and carefully using a straight stitch. The outer edge of your trim needs to align exactly with the selvage's edge. If you align it correctly, the trim will blend with no crookedness with your fabric.

Ribbon is one of the best trim choices to cover your selvage because it creates a beautiful "frame" to your treatment fabric. Choose trim to add contrast and pick up another color in your room's decor. For an informal treatment, choose a simple one-color trim, like grosgrain ribbon. For a more formal look, choose satin ribbon, a flat braid or picot-edge braid, a short-skirted fringe, or even a lace edging (make sure the lace's design is opaque enough to cover the selvage with no show-through).

Trying shower curtain rings and grommets

Shower curtain hooks are the metal or plastic rings that you usually use to hang shower curtains. They come in many different designs — some plain and modern, and some very ornate with a baroque feel — so you're sure to find a set that complements your window treatment. You can use them in place of rings with clips if you create small holes at the top of your panel and reinforce them with *grommets,* which are round metal rings that create sealed holes in fabric and are easy to do.

Pick up a grommet kit at any crafts or fabric store; these kits include a special grommet-setting tool. The grommets usually come eight to a kit and are available in many sizes, so pick one that looks good with your treatment — the longer and wider the curtain or drapery, the larger the grommet. Most grommets are silver or chrome color, but you may find gold tone, too.

Match your grommet size to your fabric thickness: The thicker the fabric, the larger the grommet size. For a heavier fabric, you may need more than one kit. You also need scissors, a good-quality hammer, and a secure work surface. Then follow these easy steps:

1. **Use a ruler to mark your grommet locations evenly across the top hem of your fabric, adding a little dot or circle with a marker or tailor's chalk.**

   Choose the interval at which you space your grommets according to your fabric's weight. For a lightweight fabric, every 6 inches is fine. For a heavyweight fabric, 3 or 4 inches may be better.

2. **Turn your fabric wrong side up and place the grommet bottom (see the directions in your kit to determine which one is the bottom piece) over your mark, and hit it with the hammer so it cuts through the fabric.**

   Doing so breaks through the fabric and creates a circle.

3. **Remove the grommet bottom and trim away the little circle of fabric that sits inside the grommet.**

4. **Restore the grommet bottom to the wrong side of the fabric and slip it through the hole so that it peeks through to the right side of the fabric.**

5. **Flip the fabric right side up with the grommet bottom in place.**

6. **Place the grommet top over the grommet bottom; your treatment fabric will be sitting between them.**

7. **Using your grommet tool and your hammer, hammer the top and bottom together.**

8. **Remove the grommet tool and check that the fit is secure.**

   If you need any clarifications, just check the directions on the package provided by the grommet company.

To hang your treatment with grommets, you don't necessarily need a rod and rings. Consider attaching small hooks or even decorative nails directly to your wall or window frame. Using a ruler or tape measure, measure the distance between each grommet and attach your nails or hooks accordingly.

Working smarter, not harder

Everyone loves shortcuts, and this section includes a few of our favorites for window treatments. Nobody notices these shortcuts after you're finished, and they make the job faster.

- Measure, cut, and iron all the folds and creases out of your fabric before you begin to sew. After you sit down at the sewing machine, you can breeze through your sewing and not waste time.

- Before you start to sew, hold the fabric up to the window or drape it over your rod or pole to double-check in the light that your fabric has no flaws and that you haven't made any holes or unnecessary cuts in the fabric. Doing this step also allows you to determine if your length and width are adequate.

- If you find you have underestimated your fabric and you don't have enough fabric to create a hem by folding fabric over and stitching, consider using Stitch Witchery or some other brand of iron-on bonding tape at the bottom to create a slimmer hem.

- When creating your curtain or drapery's rod sleeve, instead of stitching, you can place safety pins across the treatment, inserting them from the wrong side. Be sure to use many and space them evenly.

- Instead of sewing the edges and hems of your fabric panel, you can use pinking shears to edge your fabric and keep it from fraying.

- If you don't want to buy curtain hooks or cup hooks to attach your tiebacks, just use a small nail. Place it inside the tieback, push it through the fabric, and just nail it into the wall. The front of the tieback fabric hides the nail.

- Tension rods are a great timesaver. To hang a basic curtain, simply thread the tension rod through the rod sleeve and adjust it inside your window frame. You don't have to bother with drills and hammers, brackets, nails, and rings. (See Chapter 4 for more on tension rods.)

- Attach your trim with a hot glue gun instead of sewing it on. Hot glue is a great way to attach fabric to fabric, because it's cheap, fast, and fun. Apply small amounts as you work and keep paper towels handy to dab any excess.

Part III
Slipcovers Made Easy

The 5th Wave   By Rich Tennant

"What a lovely slipcover. I've never seen one made from parachute material."

In this part . . .

Do you want to make a new slipcover for your tired sofa or loveseat but don't own a sewing machine, or don't want to spend much time in front of one? Or conversely, do you love your handy-dandy Singer and want to use it to whip up fast but gorgeous slipcovers for nearly any piece of furniture in your home? Everything you wanted to know about making easy, inexpensive, and beautiful slipcovers is here for your perusal. The projects in this section are all easy, fun, and fast.

We also offer you some sound construction advice — from calculating your fabric needs and measuring and making patterns for your furniture's parts, to choosing great-looking accessories, preventing slippage, and fixing those little sewing flaws. This part gives you a clear idea of what makes a successful slipcover.

Chapter 10

Calculating, Measuring, and More: General Tips for Slipcovering

- -

In This Chapter

▶ Taking furniture measurements

▶ Cutting and sewing your fabric

▶ Figuring out how much fabric you need

▶ Determining seam allowance, hem allowance, and tuck-ins

▶ Whipping up a pattern

▶ Finding the right fit

- -

*O*ne of the most important parts of planning your slipcover project is measuring your furniture correctly. You need to understand the different parts of your slipcover and how they come together to make your slipcover properly, and measuring them is the beginning step in that understanding.

You also need to know how to properly determine how much fabric you need. Calculating your fabric needs informs your fabric choice in two ways: available quantity and price. Finding the right fabric in the right amount and within a budget you can live with are both crucial steps. (Check out Chapter 6 for more info. Many of the same measuring and fabric preparation concepts that we discuss there for window treatments are applicable to slipcover making.)

In this chapter, you discover all about measuring, cutting, and constructing your slipcover. We also give you advice on how to determine your total fabric quantities, offer some fitting tips, and show you how to make an easy pattern so you can make your slipcover right the first time.

Measuring Furniture and Cutting and Sewing Fabric for Slipcovers

This section provides some valuable information when you begin measuring your furniture and then when you pull out the scissors and needle and thread. Keep these ideas in mind when you start thinking about making your project.

Measuring tips

For each project in this book, we offer specific measuring instructions to make your life as easy as possible. However, making correct measurements for slipcovers can be tricky because slipcovers need so much fabric. The following list offers a few general tips to help you:

- **Always allow for extra yardage, just in case you need it.** Cutting off an extra ½ or ¾ yard of fabric is easier than having to go back to the fabric store, locate your bolt, and buy more. In the worst-case scenario, your bolt is gone, the fabric is no longer available from the manufacturer, and you have to start all over again. You definitely don't want that to happen! Buy the little extra yardage. You can always use whatever you have left over to cover a matching pillow, or to make a contrasting tieback for a window treatment in the same room.

- **When measuring unusually shaped furniture, measure at the largest dimension both vertically and horizontally.** If you have a sofa that is wider on top than at the bottom, measuring along the widest part can ensure you have adequate coverage. Be sure to add in your ½-inch seam allowance on each edge (or 1 inch, if you prefer), and for "bottom" pieces of your furniture that will be hemmed, be sure to add a 1- to 1½-inch allowance so you have plenty of fabric to construct your hem.

Always use a soft, cloth tape measure so you can correctly gauge the wraparound sections of your furniture, and to tuck into your sofa's or chair's crevices for tuck-ins, if necessary (see "Calculating Seam Allowance, Hem Allowance, and Tuck-ins" for more info). A metal tape measure doesn't account for the "give" you need for slipcovers.

Cutting and sewing tips

The biggest sewing challenge you face when making slipcovers is how to manage the large amount of fabric you have to maneuver through the sewing machine. These few tips can help: